DATE DUE

SEP 19 1995	

BRODART   Cat. No. 23-221

COLD IRON AND LADY GODIVA

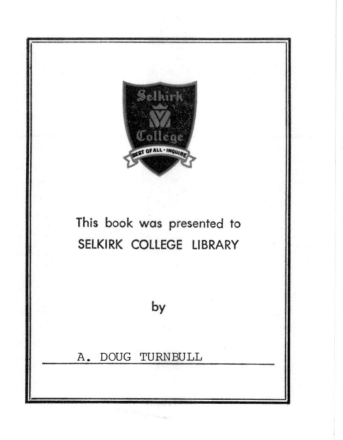

EDITED BY ROBIN S. HARRIS AND IAN MONTAGNES

Cold Iron and Lady Godiva

Engineering Education at Toronto 1920-1972

UNIVERSITY OF TORONTO PRESS

© University of Toronto Press
Toronto and Buffalo
Printed in Canada

ISBN 0-8020-2062-3
LC 73-81756

Contents

Introduction

This volume is published to mark the centenary of the Faculty of Applied
Science and Engineering of the University of Toronto. It is not a detailed
history of the Faculty nor is it a systematic assessment of the achievements
of the Faculty during the first one hundred years of its life. The objective
is a much more modest one, one which can perhaps best be described as
an attempt to take stock – to establish in general outline the course which
the Faculty has pursued since its establishment (though particularly during
the past fifty years), to define, again in general terms, its present position,
and to indicate the directions in which it is headed as it begins its second
century of service to the university of which it is an integral part, the province which provides the bulk of its funds, the profession which determines
its terms of reference, and the nation whose welfare is its ultimate goal. Col-
lectively our authors have been set the task of answering four questions:
what exactly is the Faculty of Applied Science and Engineering at the
University of Toronto? what does it do? how has it evolved to the position
it occupies in 1973? what has it meant to be a student in the Faculty at particular points in time? As might be expected since more than a single author
is involved, a number of answers rather than a single one are produced by
these questions. However, a single impression does emerge from the pages
which follow, albeit one with many parts – a complexity hinted at in the
title of this book. The engineer is more than a graduate and practitioner.
'Cold Iron' symbolizes his calling and the ring he wears, 'Lady Godiva' his
undergraduate life, his zest, his innovation and – for let us not forget the
reason for her ride – his active sense of involvement in his community's
affairs.

Nine of the ten chapters are concerned primarily with the period since 1920, the tenth, Dean Ham's, with the decade of the 1970s. This does not reflect a lack of interest in the first half century of the Faculty's life nor any lack of awareness of the strength and continuing significance of the traditions which were established between 1873 and 1919. However, there is already in print an excellent study of this formative period, C.R. Young's *Early Engineering Education at Toronto, 1851–1919,* published by the University of Toronto Press in 1958. *Cold Iron and Lady Godiva* will prove a much richer experience if it is preceded by a reading or a re-reading of *Early Engineering Education at Toronto.*

The committee which planned and authorized this volume gave serious consideration to commissioning a study comparable to Young's for the period since 1920. It reluctantly abandoned this possibility on discovering that there simply was not enough time for such a history to be completed for publication during the centennial year. It is to be hoped that a companion volume to Young's will be published at the time of the celebration of the sesquicentennial of the University of Toronto in 1977.

Technically speaking the centenary of the Faculty of Applied Science and Engineering will occur in the year 2000 since it was not until 4 December 1900 that a Faculty of Applied Science and Engineering of the University of Toronto was constituted by a statute of the University Senate, but it can also be argued that the proper year to celebrate the centenary is 2006 since it was not until 1906 that the Faculty ceased to be the financial responsibility of the Ontario government and became an integral part of the University of Toronto. Indeed a case can be made that the effective date marking the emergence of the Faculty as an educational institution occurred in 1871, 1872, 1878, 1881, 1884, 1886, 1889, or 1893. The 'correct' date depends upon one's definition of the Faculty.

What *is* the Faculty of Applied Science and Engineering of the University of Toronto? It has had this name since 1900 but the institution had by that time been operating for many years, first as the College of Technology (authorized by the Legislature of the Province on 14 February 1871) and from 1873 as the School of Practical Science. Instruction was first offered in 1872 but there were no full-time students until 1878. The first member of staff, W.H. Ellis, was appointed in 1872 but there was no professor of engineering until 1878. Nor until 1878 when the little red Schoolhouse was constructed on the university campus was there a 'permanent' building. There were no alumni until 1881 when J.L. Morris was awarded the first diploma of the School of Practical Science. The University of Toronto degree was first awarded to a graduate of SPS in 1886 following the authorization of the professional degree of civil engineer by the Senate of the university in 1884. It was not until 1889 that the School of Practical Science was formally affiliated with the University of Toronto. The four-year course leading to the B A SC degree was not authorized until 1891 and this degree was not awarded until 1893.

The question of when the Faculty began cannot be answered until one has decided what the Faculty is. Is it the teaching staff (an argument for 1872)? Is it the students (1872 or, if one insists upon full-time students, 1878)? Is it a course of study clearly recognized to be at university level (1878)? Is it a course of study which someone has completed (1881) or which leads to a recognized degree (1884 or 1891)? Is it a building (1872 or 1878)? Is it an organizational structure – a council, a principal or dean, a secretary, or an office (1872 or 1878 or 1889)? Is it an organization formally (1889) or organically (1906) related to the larger complex that is the University of Toronto?

To each of these questions the answer is yes. The Faculty of Applied Science and Engineering is a body of students (undergraduate, graduate, postdoctoral, full-time, part-time), it is a body of staff members (academic, non-academic, full-time, part-time, emeritus), it is a body of alumni (in 1973 some seventeen thousand strong), it is a complex of buildings (at Gull Lake in the Haliburton district as well as on the St George campus), it is a collection of degree and diploma courses, it is an organizational structure (the Council) but also a *network* of organizational structures (Council, departments, Engineering Society, Alumni Association). It is also an entity that is an organic part of the University of Toronto and one that has functional relationships with faculties of engineering at other Ontario and Canadian universities and with the profession of engineering in Canada. It is each of these things at one and the same time. It is not, however, an easy matter to deal with all the components at one and the same time, and for this reason particular elements – the teaching staff, the students, the alumni, the organizational structure – are the focus of attention in the chapters which follow.

As indicated earlier, this book is designed to raise and answer certain questions. This introduction centres upon the question, what is the Faculty of Applied Science and Engineering of the University of Toronto? The authors of the first three chapters are concerned with the development of the Faculty from 1920 to the present: Professor Hughes with the curriculum, both undergraduate and graduate, and with the increasingly complex organizational structure of the Council and the departments; Professor MacElhinney with student organizations; and W.W. Walker and A.M.

Reid with the Engineering Alumni Association. The second section provides four answers to the question, what was it like to be a student in the Faculty at a particular point in time: the 1920s (A.M. Reid), during the depression (R.S. Segsworth), at Ajax (A.M. Heisey), in 1971–2 (Eric Miglin). The following chapters ask what the Faculty has achieved: Professor Etkin with respect to the teaching staff, Philip Lapp with respect to the alumni. In his concluding chapter Dean Ham considers the immediate future: what are the demands which will be made upon the Faculty during the next ten to twenty years, and how well is it prepared to deal with them.

ROBIN S. HARRIS

June 1973

COLD IRON AND LADY GODIVA

P.B. HUGHES

The Faculty

John Galbraith died in the summer of 1914, full of honour; he had been appointed professor of civil engineering in 1878, coincident with the translation of the five-year-old Ontario School of Practical Science from its downtown site (the northeast corner of Church and Adelaide Streets) to the precincts of the university; in this appointment, successively changed to professor of engineering, principal, and dean, he was continuously until his death head of SPS and its successor, the Faculty of Applied Science and Engineering. The thirty-six years of Galbraith's tenure largely moulded the character and to a degree the lineaments of the Faculty as it now is.

Some historians have it that the Victorian era ended with the summer of 1914. We are tempted to look back on that fateful year as a point of contraflexure in the time rate of change of the human condition, to think that here we must perceive the first evidence of the exponential nature of a curve whose steepness in our own days is all too visible. But no such sharply defined point can in fact be fixed. The first world war did indeed bring instant changes in the human condition, in Canada as elsewhere – the terrible perturbations of war followed by the expedients of recovery – but at the beginning of the twenties we find, as Creighton put it in *Dominion of the North,* that 'the Dominion, which appeared in 1919 to face a new world order, had sunk back comfortably into the habits of the past.' Similarly, the life of the Faculty, once the immediate effects of the war had subsided, showed no dramatic point of change. The Galbraith era, which to me seems logically to extend to the retirement of Dean Ellis in 1919, merged quietly into the half-century with which this chapter is concerned.

Because mechanical engineering rather than history is my natural mode, I have reverted to the draftsman's medium for conveying information and have set forth a good deal of factual information in the 'instant history' plot of figure 1. What I write is one man's perception of the course of change, which, needless to say, will not be the perception of every man. In describing that change as a gradual process, I can at least summon support from one of Sidney Smith's presidential addresses: 'Change within a university encounters all the difficulties of moving a cemetery; universities do not act precipitately.'

Charles Hamilton Mitchell, a practising civil engineer who had been attached to British Intelligence during the later stages of the war with the rank of Brigadier General, was appointed to succeed Dean Ellis. The appointment, like that of Sir Arthur Currie to the principalship of McGill, was no doubt prompted by the wish to honour and to obtain the services of men of proven capacity and at the same time to provide for a fresh examination of the functions and functioning of the institution concerned. Neither of these eminent soldiers had direct academic experience save as undergraduates, although Mitchell, who was of the sps Class of '92, had served prior to the war on both the Senate and the Board of Governors.

The Faculty Council over which General Mitchell presided in 1919 was a redoubtable lot: Angus, Bain, Gillespie, Guess, Haultain, Rosebrugh, Stewart, C.H.C. Wright – all men of strong character; and the members of Council from the Faculty of Arts, who participated vigorously, such as E.F. Burton, A.T. DeLury, and Lash Miller, can be similarly described. Mitchell seems to have kept the peace of Council with wisdom and austerity. There can be little doubt of his command of a student body consisting of over 50 per cent soldiers (the common term for what we would now call veterans) and no doubt at all of the high respect in which, through all his twenty-two years as dean, he was held by the university, by the public, and by the engineering profession. He assumed no substantial teaching duties; no student legends had their origin in him.

The staff of the Faculty was strong not only in the character of its senior members but in the closeness of all its members to their own branches of the profession and in their common devotion to the end expressed in the sps Act of 1873: 'practical education in such arts as mining, engineering, mechanics and manufactures ... to promote the development of the mineral and economic resources of the Province, and its industrial progress.' Throughout the succeeding years, that devotion to the objective formulated in 1873 has remained. At the same time change in the notion of what constitutes practical education within a university has also been consistently evident.

The aftermath of the first world war was very different from that of the second. In 1920, demobilization of the forces did no more than restore undergraduate strength to what it had been in 1911; by 1925, registration had fallen to its lowest point since 1903. It is true that, starting in 1919, 43,000 veterans were supported in retraining by 'Soldiers' Civil Re-establishment,' but of these only 3,200 went to universities. In contrast, the retraining figures after the second world war were 134,000, with 54,000 at universities. In the twenties the habits of the past with respect to who went to universities still prevailed.

Dean Mitchell, in his annual report for the academic year 1925-6, wrote that 'the full effect of the increased standards of entrance has been felt ... signs are not wanting of a steady though slight increase ... the [economic] tide has turned.' The increased standard to which the dean referred came into effect in 1923; English and mathematics at honour matriculation level were required in addition to the normal range of pass matriculation subjects. It is surprising today to note that among the latter, physics and chemistry (then called experimental science) were optional and not a requisite for admission to the Faculty.

During the 1925-6 session, 445 undergraduates and nine graduates were enrolled in the Faculty. The teaching staff numbered thirty of professorial rank, thirteen lecturers, and thirty-nine sessional appointees. In 1920-1, for a registration of slightly over eight hundred, the comparable teaching staff numbers had been twenty-three, none, and fifty-five. Time lags always exist in a business as meticulous as appointing professors – and mistakes in prognostication did not begin with the advent of the computer. However, nine of the 1925-6 professors were listed in the President's Report as publishing articles or books, while in 1920-1 the same listing showed only three. The easing of the teaching load seems to have had what today we would call a wholesome effect. Yet forty years ago such an opinion would have been expressed only with caution. Sir Robert Falconer, then president, whose intellectual vigour was of the first order, wrote in his report for the year 1930–1:

In looking over the period since the war it is evident that the School of Graduate Studies has assumed a position of great importance in the University. Not less so, indeed concomitantly, has interest developed in research. So universal has it become that it is almost invidious to single out individuals and departments. *Many of these researches seem to have little direct bearing on life, though perhaps most are in subjects which may be applied in medicine or mechanical affairs.*

The italic is mine. The contrast with Sidney Smith's statement in his 1947-8 report (and it is the times I place in contrast, not the men) is marked:

It is the duty of the University to attract to and retain on its staff a group of able men and women equipped both to inspire and guide ... and also to discover new facts and principles. A teacher can only be a gifted teacher if his mind is alive and alert to new viewpoints in his chosen field ... 'He who learns from one who has learned all he has to teach "drinks the dark mantle of a stagnant pool."'

In 1920-1, the 'General First Year' (a common first year for all courses except Architecture and Chemical) was dropped. The same session saw the demise of the original Course 5, Analytical Chemistry, as distinct from Chemical Engineering. For the next thirteen years there were seven courses in which students might pursue their B A SC degrees: 1/Civil, 2/Mining, 3/Mechanical, 4/Architecture, 6/Chemical, 7/Electrical, 8/Metallurgical. Divided among these (figure 1 indicates the varying proportions) was an undergraduate body that had increased by the session of 1930-1 to a record strength of 850, far exceeding the dean's cautious prediction of 1926. By the end of that session the dean was expressing alarm at the threatened imbalance between applicants for Chemical and the available laboratory facilities, and in his annual report he raised the possibility of directing or controlling enrolment in order to keep course strengths commensurate with facilities, but suggested no system for doing so. In fact, it is only in recent years and at the level of about 2,000 students that a degree of control of the student's choice has been necessary; this has been applied mainly at the time of registration in first year.

Courses have waxed and waned in popularity in a manner not easy to explain. There is a psychological momentum in those emerging from high school (Johnny is predisposed to what his friend or hero of last year did) and at different periods the public notion of the future favours one specialization or another. Over the long run, it is the courses which lead to practice in a professional area, rather than those which lead to employment in a particular industry, that have thrived.

A significant change came in the session 1934-5 with the introduction of Engineering Physics, which adopted the number 5 left vacant by the demise of Analytical Chemistry. The new course was described, with rather more than becoming modesty, in the calendar of that session as giving 'a training

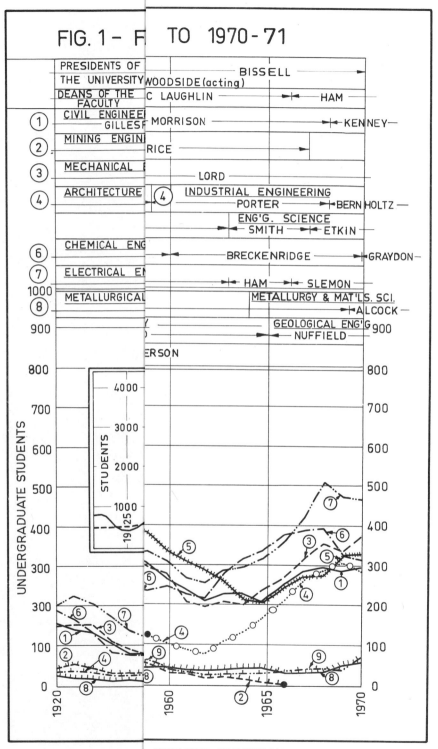

FIG. 1 – F TO 1970-71

MECHANICAL ENGINEERING   P. B. H. / B. EHRICH

in Mathematics and Physics beyond that which it is possible to give in the other undergraduate courses in Engineering ... [to achieve] a readier appreciation of technical problems and a greater facility in the solution of them.' The course required, and still requires, a higher scholastic standing for entry than the other courses; special fields were and are still followed, initially in the fourth year and, since 1936-7, in the third year as well. The change in name to Engineering Science was made in 1962-3 in recognition of the fact that all fields of science fall within its purview.

The establishment of Engineering Physics marked a change in the interpretation of the 1873 Act – 'practical education in the arts of mining, engineering, mechanics and manufactures' – a change that had already, and subtly, begun to affect the curricula of the departments before that time and that has become less subtle, and indeed widely recognized, in the ensuing years. The evidence appears in the gradual reduction of the time given to the teaching of subjects of 'vocational utility' (E.W.R. Steacie's term) or practical skills, and the increased time and weight given to more fundamental subjects. This change in the view of practical education is perhaps the dominant characteristic of the fifty years of history here considered; perhaps, too, the change would be better described by saying that the 'vocational utility' or 'tool' subjects of instruction have not been reduced in favour of the fundamental, but that they themselves have changed: the fundamentals have become the 'tool' subjects of engineering practice. We must remember, if some measure of criticism of the past is inferred from what has been said, that Galbraith was himself a gold medallist in Maths and Physics and that his staff were mostly of comparable academic background. Practical application was always, both in SPS and in the Faculty, developed on a solid ground of fundamentals. But today the range of fundamentals is vastly greater, practical application is less easily codified, and the traditional instruction in the practical is much curtailed.

Mining Geology (Course 9) was inaugurated in 1937, with an initial registration of ten students. Dean Mitchell thus described it in his annual report that year: 'It is not an engineering course, but is essentially one in applied science designed to better fit graduates specializing in geological science to understand and appreciate the problems of mining engineers.' The administrative heads of this course, successively E.S. Moore, G.B. Langford, and E.W. Nuffield, have all been professors of geology in the Faculty of Arts. The name of the course has been changed successively to Applied Geology (in 1953) and to Geological Engineering (in 1965), and, the original description notwithstanding, the course has thrived since its inception as one addressed to an area of engineering practice.

Dean Mitchell noted in his annual report for 1936-7 a change in a two-year option in Metallurgical, previously called Ceramics, to a four-year option, still within Metallurgical, to be known as Ceramics and Non-Metallic Industrial Minerals. This deserves a glance backwards and a glance ahead. In 1925 the original Ceramics option was introduced with enthusiasm in the Dean's Report as 'long desired and ... made possible by the generous financial help of the Canadian Clay Products Association ... Great attention ... has been directed toward this University on entering this new field.' This was an example of an out-and-out industry-oriented specialization, complete with funding by the industry. By 1951, however, Dean K.F. Tupper was reporting: 'For many years this course has attracted a very small number of students. Moreover, there seems to be little reason to continue to offer a specialized course to meet the demands of this one industry.' The option was discontinued. Five years later Dean R.R. McLaughlin made what might be called the definitive statement about 'specialization-by-industry'; this will be quoted later.

The last Dean's Report before the outbreak of war (by C.H. Mitchell in June 1939) spoke of changes in the curriculum made 'in a desire to anticipate the requirements for suitably educated young men going out into engineering and business fields, which have materially changed in the past decade. The technical requirements of today impose many new subjects which ten or twenty years ago were not in the applied science picture; nowadays engineering education has come to be a mosaic of a complicated and multi-coloured pattern.' The dean was referring to the fact that a total of 269 lecture courses and 189 laboratory courses, 458 in all, were listed in the calendar for the forthcoming session (1939-40, in which the registration turned out to be 961) – a 50 per cent increase in the number of courses from ten years before when there were 701 undergraduates, while the academic staff increased over the ten years only from 49 to 60. There was, as the dean noted, a trend toward increasing professorial work loads. Fortunately the proliferation of subjects of instruction has not continued at the same rate: in 1971-2 (with an undergraduate registration of 2,238) the Faculty offered some 570 undergraduate subjects, many of them options, and the staff (professors of all ranks and lecturers) numbered about 165.

Two remarks are in order here. First, the figures cited should not be simply taken to indicate greater or smaller staff teaching loads at any period. The graduate student, as will later be shown, is an increasingly significant factor and class-size variations also affect any such comparison. Second, there has been a change of language in recent years. Subjects of instruction are now courses, and what were called courses (e.g., Civil Engineering) are now called programs. There is still some inconsistency in our usage of the terms.

During the second world war enrolment in the Faculty generally rose, in marked contrast with the period 1914-18. Students and prospective students were encouraged by the government to complete or to undertake courses in science and engineering, for it was clear that the useful man in the new warfare was the man trained in arts not previously required of the soldier. The President's Reports for 1939-40 and 1940-1, and Dean Mitchell's reports contained therein, dealt with distractions and expedients arising from the war; they are a record of quiet service in a field remote from the great theatres of history. The men were keen to put their new talents to work: President H.J. Cody, in June 1943, reported that 'Graduating classes frequently enlist, virtually *en masse*.' The staff, both of the Faculty and of the university, also was depleted by enlistment; most of those who remained picked up additional burdens and swallowed courageously what General Eisenhower (at Stormont, Northern Ireland, in 1945) called '... the bitter draft of him whose duty it is to send other men into peril and death.'

Dean Mitchell's report for the 1940-1 session was his last before retirement. He spoke warmly of his associates, and warmly also of his appointed successor, C.R. Young, whom he described as a man of 'fine administrative ability, long university experience and wide professional prestige.' Read quickly, the words have a rhetorical sound, but any who knew C.R. Young will recognize them as reasoned statements. His firm and gentle leadership was a major factor in the Faculty's development and accomplishments during the next eight years.

Aeronautical Engineering was instituted in the 1944-5 session under T.R. Loudon, also head of Civil, newly returned from active service. Loudon had graduated with honours in 1905; his contemporaries, F.W. Baldwin and J.A.D. McCurdy, had taken their degrees in 1906 and 1907 respectively and had become, in association with Dr Alexander Graham Bell, the pioneers of powered flight in Canada. One can imagine the intensity of interest in aeronautics in their undergraduate years, when the Wright brothers were in the process of making history, Bleriot was contemplating his cross-Channel flight, and the world was accustoming itself to the notion that it might one day be possible to fly a hundred miles or more. Loudon never lost this interest, and in his field of applied mechanics was a consultant to civil and military aviation all his life.

Aeronautical studies at Toronto evolved gradually. The first instruction was given, and the first wind tunnel constructed, by J.H. Parkin in the Department of Mechanical Engineering during the early thirties. After Parkin left the staff, to take up what proved to be a distinguished career in science, some optional 'aero' subjects were offered in Civil and Mechanical. In 1935, aeronautical became an option in Engineering Physics.

The full new course in Aeronautical Engineering accepted undergraduates only for nine years. During the 1954-5 session, some five years after the establishment of the Institute of Aerophysics under G.N. Patterson, 'aero' again became an option in Engineering Physics, leading to graduate level studies at the Institute (now the Institute for Aerospace Studies). Since 1954, Toronto has not offered a full program in aeronautical engineering at the bachelor level.

A letter of historic import was addressed on 16 November 1944 by Dean Young to Sidney Smith, then principal of University College and president-designate of the university. It was accompanied by a brief prepared by W.J.T. Wright, broaching the question of how the Faculty was to handle the unprecedented registration to be expected on demobilization of the forces. Between that date and January 1946, the enormous task of providing the organization and facilities of Ajax was accomplished. The university and the government provided co-operation, decision, action, and money, and these of the all-but-instant variety. As to the Faculty, for any who have watched its Council strain over the gnats of more normal times, the camel-swallowing that must have gone on during that period is wonderful to contemplate.

The site of the Ajax Division was part of 3,600 acres occupied by a shell-filling plant constructed during the war about twenty-five miles east of Toronto. One hundred and eleven buildings were taken over on 428 acres; these buildings, already heated and serviced with power and sewers, were converted, improved, and furnished so as to constitute a self-contained academic community. Between 14 January 1946 and 31 May 1949, 5,500 students (of whom 3,500 were veterans) entered the university through this portal. They took their first and, for a time, second years in these anything-but-ivy-covered halls, and then transferred to the St George Campus.

To meet their numbers, the teaching staff grew, but not commensurately with the demands upon it. The strain is suggested in an overly modest report, 'Engineering Education for ex-Servicemen,' dated January 1950, by W.J.T. Wright, who was director of studies at Ajax (assisted by H.L. Shepherd), from which the data on teaching staff in table 1 have been extracted.

The teaching staff of the Faculty of Arts, whose participation is not included in the figures above, contributed generously and enthusiastically. The non-academic staff of the university also brought efficiency and

TABLE 1

	Average 1935–45	The peak 1947–8	1949–50
Professors – all grades	41.3	49	54
Lecturers	12.5	59	36
Instructors & demonstrators (full-time equivalent)	45.6	137	100
Total Full-time	99.4	245	190
Part-time lecturers	13.7	33	55

warmth of co-operation to this massive departure from their normal operations. If co-operation, decision, action, and money were the prime dynamics of the inception of Ajax, unselfish and unremitting devotion to the undertaking of restoring something of the lost years to the veterans was the sustaining spirit.

The initiation of the course in Engineering and Business in 1946 gave somewhat hesitant recognition to management-administration as a field of legitimate and increasingly common employment for engineers, and thus one in which a specialization should be offered. Independent surveys carried out by the Engineering Alumni Association and the Engineering Institute of Canada had indicated that about 50 per cent of graduate engineers were engaged in administrative work, production, or sales, 'with some engineering content.' In proposing the course to Council, Dean Young referred to the experience of MIT, which had taken the step thirty years earlier. In his brief one perceives the collaboration of E.A. Allcut, who had recently succeeded R.W. Angus as head of Mechanical, and was himself an able exponent both of engineering and management.

Objections were made in Council to the effect that the new course would be a reversion to out-and-out vocational training, and that there was no discernible academic discipline involved but only a sequence of elementary studies. These objections were overborne. Perhaps the clinching argument – a strong one at the time – was that such a type of training would be well suited to 'many men who will be discharged from the armed forces or released from war industries.' Perhaps also Council was impressed by the fact that such a course was being offered by nineteen fully accredited engineering schools in the United States. In any case, the first registration of forty students took place in 1946.

The planning that brought Ajax into being extended to meet the subsequent heavy attendance on the St George Campus. The new Mechanical Building and the Wallberg Building were constructed so as to be ready for occupation in the session 1949-50, just in time for the return to Toronto of the students from Ajax, which brought the St George Campus attendance in the Faculty to a record number of 2,904 undergraduates. Even with the new space it was necessary to start the working days at 8 am, and some laboratories carried on until 9 pm.

The two new buildings represented a departure in character from what was traditionally considered appropriate for an engineering school. Except for the imaginative bas-reliefs of the Schoolhouse (properly known as the Engineering Building, but commonly by this affectionate nickname) previous fabrics had been stark. Panelled and glazed tile walls provided a welcome contrast to dusty plaster and unpainted brick; in exterior form and embellishment, as well as in their arrangement, the new buildings were modern. The staff and student common rooms (E.A. Allcut's far-sighted idea) in the Mechanical Building were novel for the south end of the campus. W.G. McIntosh, professor of machine design, collaborated with the architects in the design of the Mechanical Building as he did some years later with those of the Galbraith Building.

A major factor in the planning and use of space, as well as in determining the teaching load of professors, is the graduate student. Up to the immediate post-Ajax session, he was a comparatively *rara avis*. In 1938-9, the Faculty had reached a record of 28 graduate students against an undergraduate registration of 960. In 1943-4, the figures were 9 and 1,200 respectively – an indication that few young men were willing to linger for extended periods in the groves of academe at that time. In 1949-50, however, 169 graduate students were registered against an undergraduate strength of 2,904. Two years later, although the number of undergraduates had fallen to 1,619, there were 125 graduate students, proportionately more in relation to undergraduates than ever before.

There are ready-use figures by which the increase in demands upon staff, facilities, and money represented by graduate students may be estimated as opposed to the demands of undergraduates alone. The difference is enormous, but it can be argued that such figures are nothing but bookkeeping expedients. Certainly, the time a professor devotes to a graduate student is so great that at first sight his emphasis seems to be withdrawn from the training of the young engineer (and from the objectives cited in the Act of 1873) and placed on the more sophisticated education in applied science of the relatively few. But this first sight is deceptive. In

an atmosphere of sophisticated study and research, the young engineer following the undergraduate curriculum is not so much putting away a pack-
age of knowledge required for his profession, as building a foundation that
will enable him to practise in the inquiring and innovative spirit he sees
around him. A paradox suggests itself here: we *teach* the graduate student
in order to *educate* the undergraduate.

The ratio of graduate students to undergraduates for 1969-70 was more
than twice what it was in 1951-2. The causes for this continuing growth are
less easy to identify, however, than they once were. They no longer simply
reflect increased access to the university, or the increasing level of scientific content in engineering. The demographic mobility that has swelled
Ontario's population since the early 1950s has brought many candidates for
higher degrees who have attained bachelor status elsewhere. Nor is it likely
that the ratio will continue to increase; indeed, the Lapp Report (*Ring of
Iron: a Report to the Committee of Presidents of the Universities of
Ontario*) recommended for Toronto a graduate student limit of 480 in
Applied Science and Engineering, as against an undergraduate limit of
2,000.

In his report for the session 1947-8, Dean Young wrote:

With regret, the Faculty ... has witnessed the separation from it of the School of
Architecture. Henceforth that School will function as a separate unit with its own
Director and Council. The Faculty ... will continue to furnish instruction in
engineering subjects to students in Architecture. It wishes the new School every
success.

This separation, after more than sixty years in which Architecture was a
part of Engineering, was probably inevitable. The specialization required
of the architect was more and more growing distinct from that of the
engineer, and there had been no approach to union at the professional level.
Although never forming a large proportion of the student body of the
Faculty, the number of students in Architecture had increased to 280 by
this time. That figure has been reasonably well sustained, and indeed has
of late been exceeded by what is now a division of a full faculty (Architecture, Urban and Regional Planning and Landscape Architecture) in its own
right.

C.R. Young retired at the end of June 1949. He continued the practice
of civil engineering, in which he was outstanding, and found time in the
years remaining before his death in 1963 to write *Early Engineering Educa-*

tion at Toronto, 1851-1919 (University of Toronto Press, 1958), to which today we largely owe our knowledge of the origins and early development of the Faculty.

Young's successor was Kenneth Tupper, who, like General Mitchell thirty years before (and like Deans J.W.B. Sisam of Forestry and C.A. Wright of Law, who were both appointed at about the same time as Tupper), represented one of the periodic infusions of new blood that are generally considered healthy for academic bodies. A graduate of 1929 who had earned his master's degree at the University of Michigan eleven years later, Tupper had had a distinguished professional career as chief engineer of Turbo Research, Ltd, a war-time Crown Corporation, and after the war at the nuclear establishment at Chalk River. He was recognized as a skilful administrator and a first-rate scientist and engineer; to his new office he brought a keen and innovative mind.

As the only living ex-dean when this chapter was written, Dr Tupper was good enough to look back on his period in office.

It was never an ambition of mine to increase the size of SPS. On the contrary, I feared that the place would grow to an unwieldy size. Even in 1949, the average student could not become acquainted with all the members of his own class, much less with students in other disciplines, and hence he completely failed to get the benefits which a university can offer. He was attending a vocational school.

I did a lot to permit entrance at the second and third year level for students who had taken pre-engineering courses at McMaster, Western and Lakehead, with the hope of reducing the Toronto enrolment ... [and] I encouraged the establishment of engineering facilities in other Ontario universities. What about quality? It soon became a belief of mine that a university could not add a cubit to any man's stature; the men who graduated were the same you had admitted some years earlier. Contemplating MIT and Caltech and their excellent performance, I noted their astonishingly low failure rates. It was obvious that they admitted only the cream of the crop, while Toronto admitted whole milk. To turn out our cream we had to turn out a second stream of skim milk. Yet in my opinion the second stream differed in kind rather than in quality or social value; they were not so bookish, or they were not really motivated towards engineering. The two-stream process is unavoidable in a university supplied by public funds. There is nothing much one can do beyond demanding higher and higher Grade XIII marks within the public support restriction.

Again, the alumni records I examined showed poor correlation with academic transcripts. The then presidents of Babcock-Wilcox, Imperial Oil, Alcan, and the general manager (later chairman) of Ontario Hydro, all graduates of the Faculty and all known to me, numbered among them only one good student – and one of them had taken five years to get his degree! Also, I noted that three of my contemporaries (one, Willson Woodside, had been my room-mate) had distinguished themselves in non-engineering fields. I talked to many such graduates who had taken up non-engineering work with success. None regretted having studied engineering, though generally they admitted that other courses would have served them as well. It seemed to me that we had not done badly for our less-than-brilliant students, and that, regarded as pure education, our operation was fair.

I never did solve the problem of academic goal, and I am no nearer to it in 1972 than I was in 1952.

Tupper resigned in 1954, expressing the opinion that, whatever the benefit of a 'new-blood' dean might be, it would have had to be gained in five years. He left, high in the esteem of his colleagues, and became in due course vice-president, scientific of the National Research Council of Canada, from which post he retired in 1971.

Roland McLaughlin, his successor, was well known throughout the university. He first came to the staff as a lecturer in Chemical Engineering in 1930, and had been head of that department since 1947. His appointment was popular. For several years after assuming the deanship he continued as head of Chemical, turning that position over to John Breckenridge only in 1960. At the end of his first year in office, McLaughlin was able to report that the struggle to work out a common first year had progressed – but not very far, for exceptions remained for four of the ten departments. The problem to which Dr Tupper referred above was also exercising McLaughlin, for he spoke of a newly-formed committee on development under G. Ross Lord, which was charged with the duty of making 'an assessment of [the Faculty's] methods, objectives and responsibilities towards the society it serves' in the light of an expected doubling of the enrolment by 1965.

This report is not quoted in an effort to evoke a smile at another enrolment prediction (the 1965 registration proved in fact to be smaller than the 1,800-odd of 1954) but to provide background for an argument debated by the dean and Sidney Smith in the dignified medium of the President's Reports. In his report for the 1954-5 session, Dr Smith commended the new arrangements for aeronautical studies but took the faculty to task with mild severity about the still only 'substantially' common first year, deplored the tendency to specialize, and questioned the division into ten undergraduate courses. In his report of the following year, however, he generously conceded the honours by quoting verbatim McLaughlin's reply, which thus appeared twice in that volume. The statement is entirely applicable today.

Specialization has a different meaning for different people. The day has long since passed when a 'general ' engineering course of four years' duration had any real meaning. Differentiation into well-known divisions such as, for example, Civil, Mechanical, Electrical and Chemical Engineering is essential. And not just for 'practical' reasons. Any university discipline, provided it goes deep enough, is good training for life. But it must be a study in depth of some one discipline. A superficial survey of a number of disciplines will not suffice. Advances in the basic sciences and in technology have brought about the situation wherein each of the major divisions of engineering is a discipline in itself and can only be pursued with profit in four years if it is so regarded. With some minor exceptions, the 'know-how' has long ago given way to the 'know-why.' We leave the accumulation of 'know-how' to practical experience in the summer months and to industry after the student has graduated. This is not only because we have not time for it but because it is better learned outside the university. And so the choosing of subjects of instruction is a hard business, having to be ground out between the upper millstone of ever increasing scientific knowledge, and the nether millstone of four short years which nowadays contain, and rightly so, a leaven of studies in the humanities. There is no temptation towards or opportunity for 'specialization' as we understand it – for example, Automotive Engineering as a subdivision of Mechanical Engineering, or Petroleum Engineering as a subdivision of Chemical Engineering.

Extrapolation of a time series is said to have one virtue; the upshot keeps us humble. The Faculty's various planning committees have had their fair share of such lessons. Nevertheless, Dean McLaughlin's potential undergraduate enrolment of 3,600 in 1965 might well have been upon us if that year's Ontario total of 5,685 engineering undergraduates had been divided in the familiar proportion of about 2:1 between Toronto and Queen's. That total in 1965-6 was in fact divided as follows: Toronto, 28%; Queen's, 17%; Waterloo, 27%; and the remainder between Carleton, McMaster, Western, Windsor, Ottawa, Guelph, Laurentian, and Lakehead. All of these except Toronto and Queen's had started granting degrees in engineering after 1955.

By 1969-70, the total undergraduate registration in engineering in Ontario had reached 8,528 and the percentage figures for Toronto, Queen's, and Waterloo were 26, 18, and 28 respectively. The new schools built upon the old. According to the Lapp Report, the degrees held by teaching staff of Ontario engineering schools in 1969-70 were 43 per cent Canadian, and of these half were from Toronto. Whatever our virtues and defects may be, they have been widely transmitted!

In January 1957 there arrived in Toronto a group of some eighty students of the University of Sopron in Hungary who, along with several hundred other students of that institution, had elected to leave their country upon the defeat of the anti-Communist revolution in 1956. The group which came to Toronto had been enrolled in courses related to geology, geophysics, and mining engineering. They were accompanied by the registrar of their faculty, Dr W. Szenci, and several of their professors. Including wives and children, the group numbered over a hundred.

The Honourable J.W. Pickersgill, then minister of citizenship and immigration, had offered the services of his department in transporting the refugees to Canada and, in advance of their arrival, had obtained assurance from the University of Toronto that the students would be admitted to undergraduate courses in engineering at levels appropriate to their qualifications. He had also negotiated with representatives of the mining industry in Canada for financial support for the group and for their eventual employment in the mining industry.

The first job was to help them learn English. The group, provided with living quarters together in order to facilitate the instruction, were the last inhabitants of the old Chorley Park mansion in north Rosedale. Stephen Davidovich of the Ontario Department of Education and Professors Robin Harris, Donald Theall, and John Wevers of the Faculty of Arts were all heavily involved in the English program. As in the Ajax days, many co-operated in this venture. By September, forty-eight of the Sopron students were enrolled in the Faculty. Twenty-nine took their degrees at Toronto, and some, transferring, graduated from other universities.

The BASC degree conferred by the university does not bear the name of the 'graduating department' which sponsors the student at Convocation. What we understand by this term is a department whose program of studies a student follows in order to achieve the degree, and such are the departments which have been mentioned up to this point. Each gives instruction in its field in some measure to students belonging to other departments. In contrast, the Faculty once had two 'teaching departments' which did not have students of their own, but, dealing with aspects of engineering well-nigh universal, taught all students. These two departments were Engineering Drawing and Applied Physics. Both have disappeared; some of the studies they gave have been curtailed, others have become specialized.

The simultaneous retirement in 1959 of W.J.T. Wright (who succeeded J. Roy Cockburn as head), and of W.B. Dunbar and A. Wardell, the department's other senior staff members, precipitated the end of Engineering Drawing and removed three familiar and well-loved figures from the undergraduate scene. Wright, who had served so well at Ajax, continued for several years as a counsellor for students. Today he acts as a wise counsellor for the like of professors who have undertaken to write histories of faculties.

Applied Physics ended with the retirement of K.B. Jackson in 1963. For some twenty-two years he was effectively head of Engineering Physics. He conceded nothing of the rigour of the demands of the course, but he infused into its students a spirit equal to the hardships they had to face, gaining vast respect and love as an unsought reward.

Somewhat analogous to the one-time teaching departments are the relatively new institutes and groups – Aerospace, Biomedical, Environmental Science, and Computer Research. These do not have undergraduate students of their own but they do give some undergraduate instruction; they are generally interdisciplinary, and their staffs include members of other faculties. They are predominantly research organizations to which graduate students are attached. Of these, the Institute for Aerospace Studies, founded in 1949, is the oldest, and has grown famous under its director, G.N. Patterson. The Institute of Biomedical Electronics, under N.F. Moody, was founded in 1962; besides conducting research common to medicine and engineering, it offers instruction in physical science for medical personnel and in the life sciences for engineers.

The Galbraith Building was opened with due ceremony in the spring of 1961. It had then been forty years since Civil and Electrical had had any increase in space. (Dean Mitchell, in 1921, had referred to the Electrical Building as the 'new building'; it had been the home of these two departments ever since.) At the same time, the old Engineering Building was assigned to a variety of uses, most of them unconnected with the Faculty. In the fall of 1966 the wreckers came for it, and the fabric of the Schoolhouse became stuff of song and story. The new Medical Sciences Building now occupies its site.

A grant to the Faculty of $2,325,000 by the Ford Foundation was announced in January 1963 for the 'strengthening of the advanced graduate program in engineering over the next five years.' Specifically, the money was given to provide about thirty graduate fellowships each year for MASC and PHD students, to make possible the appointment of senior research fellows and visiting professors, to buy research equipment, to pay for major changes at Aerospace, and to build expanded quarters for Metallurgy and Materials Science in a new wing on the northeast corner of the Wallberg Building; in addition, a large sum was to be expended at the dean's discretion. The foundation's judgment of the capacity of the Faculty for advanced research is clear – one sees the grant as help to those who already help themselves.

The long-term effect of such a grant derives largely from a mechanism of seeding – the putting out of money for initial support of new activities or the extension of existing ones, in either case undertakings that seem likely to develop so as to be competitive with other activities for whatever support may be available after the termination of the grant. New and promising work so brought to light tends to displace work that is lagging; the depth and sophistication of what is attempted increase, and the flow of public money into research is encouraged. The ramifications are wide and complex. The degree of success achieved by this handsome gift will be assessable only after the passage of many years.

In his report for 1958-9, Dean McLaughlin announced that a new graduating department, Industrial Engineering, would begin operation in the next session and that Engineering and Business would be discontinued. The specialized knowledge of the new course, he said, 'may be best described as applied mathematics.' Of the reasons for dropping the old course, he explained:

This desirable union of two fields of interest cannot be satisfactorily combined in a four-year course. It ... is impossible to maintain the engineering content at a level consistent with ... [our] aims and at the same time include the quantity of 'business' subjects naturally desired by those responsible for that part of the programme. Furthermore, twice as many students from the 'conventional' courses in the Faculty go on to graduate work in Business Administration as do students from Engineering and Business, indicating that ... students are quite willing to invest another two years in that pursuit after obtaining an engineering degree.

A factor in the criticism levelled at Engineering and Business, both in committee and later in the Faculty Council, was that its students were receiving less than justice in a *milieu* in which their fellows in other courses were undertaking increasingly sophisticated work in their various specialized fields. The capacity of these students to handle the far more formidable curriculum of Industrial Engineering was witnessed in the transition years, when students who had started in the old course switched to the new without excessive shedding of tears.

The applied mathematics of which the dean spoke included the first full-strength mathematical statistics given undergraduates in the Faculty, an intimate contact with the computer, and the constituent mathematical techniques of the recondite areas of operations research. Arthur Porter, previously dean of engineering at the University of Saskatchewan, was the first head of Industrial Engineering. To him I attribute the statement that the course would be 'directed towards the reinstatement of the engineer as the prime exponent of the analytical mind in industry.' I suggest that the changes in name and content were exactly the sort of development that E.A. Allcut, who originally advocated and for twelve years directed 'Eng-Biz,' foresaw as coming in the fullness of time. It was a development that may have sacrificed something of immediate utility for current practice, but has gained much in the searching light of a paradox posed by Sidney Smith: 'The purpose of education is not to prepare youth for their occupations, but to prepare them against their occupations.'

The Faculty opened a new chapter in service to the world-wide community in June 1963, when three of its professors travelled to India to teach at and assist in the development of the Karnataka Regional Engineering College at Sreenivasnagar, on the Arabian Sea near Mangalore, under an arrangement with the External Aid Office of Canada. The first party consisted of C.F. Morrison, G.R. Slemon, and I.W. Smith, all with their wives and families. Morrison and Slemon were relieved in the following year by C.A. Wrenshall and A. Straughen; and in 1965 Smith and Wrenshall were replaced by D.G. Huber (then on the staff of McMaster University) and J.D. Barber. All had returned to Canada by the end of 1966. Later, certain members of the KREC staff attended graduate school here as part of the scheme.

The impact of this mission is difficult to assess, but one product was the publication of a report, *Engineering Education in India,* by I.W. Smith which has since been widely used to assess the qualifications of Indian engineers coming to Canada and the USA. Whatever the benefits, the Faculty was unsparing in its loan of such men.

In his report for 1964-5, the dean announced that the undergraduate course in Mining was to be discontinued:

On many grounds this was a hard decision to reach, for the beginnings of this course stretch back almost to the foundation in 1878 of the School of Practical Science ... The enrolment has decreased almost to the vanishing point ... [but] of much greater importance is the great change that has occurred in engineering education over the past thirty years or so whereby 'training' for a specific industry is now obsolete, and has been replaced by a study in depth of some one discipline intended to extend the mental capacity of the student. I am satisfied ... that 'training' for the mineral industry is incompatible with the later objective ... much research work of direct interest to the mineral industry ... [is] going on at the graduate level in several departments of the Faculty ... [which], plus the revised course in Geological Engineering will, in my view, make a much greater contribution to the mineral industry than would maintaining the status quo in a changed and changing environment.

In 1966, Roland McLaughlin retired. His colleagues' regret was tempered by his immediate appointment to a new post as chairman of the planning division of the university. In addition to the warm good wishes of the Faculty, he carried with him a mariner's compass which John Breckenridge, presenting it on behalf of the staff, described as the instrument planning groups at Toronto were most in need of.

He was succeeded by James M. Ham, B A SC of 1943, veteran of two years' service as an Electrical Officer in the Royal Canadian Navy, SM and SC D of MIT, who was first appointed to the staff of the Faculty as an assistant professor in Electrical Engineering in 1951, and became head of that department, succeeding Gordon Tracy, in the session 1964-5. To Ham we can apply that highest of nautical assessments: he has both brains and ballast.

J. Roy Cockburn, a member of the staff for nearly sixty years, long-time head of the Department of Engineering Drawing, veteran of two wars (Lieutenant-Colonel, MC), died in 1964, and left a fortune of some half a million dollars for the use of the Faculty. The Faculty Council decided that the income from this large sum could most effectively be used in promoting that greatest art of engineering, design. Engineers, wrote Adam Smith in *The Wealth of Nations,* are 'philosophers, or men of speculation, whose trade it is not to do anything but to observe all things, and who are thereby often enabled to combine together the powers of the most distant and dissimilar objects.' Our 'studies in depth,' so frequently mentioned by presidents and deans, by which we 'observe all things,' have received increasing attention, but the 'combining together' (what I have ventured to call the greatest art of engineering) has had shorter shrift in our curricula. The Cockburn Unit in Engineering Design, with I.W. Smith as Cockburn professor and six Cockburn associates, was formed in 1968 with these objectives: 'to promote and develop engineering design, innovative skills and entrepreneurial expertise at all levels within the Faculty.' It has initiated teaching innovations, competitions, projects voluntarily undertaken by students, and liaison with industry, and is in full activity at this time.

When students of the sixties are judged by history, there will be other things to record than protests and confrontations and the decline of manners – none of which, indeed, has been widespread in the professional schools at Toronto. There have been other changes in attitude that are healthy. Notably, a larger proportion of students than formerly are prepared to think and act independently.

In January 1970, Douglas Venn, then a Master of Engineering candidate, attended a symposium of the Society of Automotive Engineers at Detroit on automobile pollution. While there, without benefit of president, board of governors, dean, or professor, he proceeded to enter the University of Toronto as a contestant in the Transcontinental Clean Air Car Race planned to run from Boston to Pasadena the following August. Venn was not, on his return, hanged, drawn, and quartered; it is not only among students that a change of attitude has occurred. Within three days, Ross Lord, having power of disposition of the unconditional bequest to the Mechanical Department known as the Wallace Estate, had authorized $10,000 (and eventually about $4,000 more) towards the building of a car; a few days later the Cockburn Unit released another $10,000; almost overnight the comptroller's office had established an appropriation account, and the game was on.

'Miss Purity' was built. The design was a mutual effort of the staff and students of Mechanical and Electrical; indeed, she was classed as 'hybrid,' since both internal combustion and an elaborate system of electrical drive were employed, all with the purpose of minimizing emissions that contribute to air pollution. She finished at Pasadena tied for first place in her class. Douglas Venn, Steve Baker, Juri Otsason, and Simon Ng were the student team that accompanied her after largely building her with their own hands with the help of the skilled tradesmen of the two departments. I.W. Smith and F.C. Hooper were the professors who rode along as advisers, and many others of the staff and student body contributed time and effort.

It was fitting that William A. Wallace, late associate professor, whose estate was the largest source of money for the project, was for years our prime expert in the automotive field. He of all men would have appreciated the value of this close student-staff collaboration.

The budget of words for this chapter is already overdrawn; we have reached 1970; it is time to stop. Of omissions, the gravest are the many names that belong in this history but have not appeared, and a sad defect is the summary manner in which so many, having momentarily entered it, have been dismissed without further account, without mention of their achievements and honours. I have been moving among giants, and I have done them all too little justice.

W.G. MACELHINNEY

The Engineering Society

Schoolmen of the past quarter-century, whose memories of their under-graduate years are enlivened by the boom of the cannon, the polyphony of the Lady Godiva Memorial Band, and the thud of peashooters during election capers at the burlesque houses on Queen Street and Spadina Avenue, may be surprised to learn that the Engineering Society, under whose sponsorship this symphony was played, originated as a 'learned society.' The circumstances of the founding of the Society, now in its eighty-eighth year, deserve to be known.

Back in 1878, when the School of Practical Science moved to the St George Street campus, its students became eligible for membership in the oldest undergraduate organization in Canada, the Literary and Scientific Society of University College, which had been established in 1854. The arrangement was a natural one since the School and the College were located only 150 yards apart and since much of the instruction offered in the School was provided by professors of the College. As Dean John Galbraith observed in 1906 in a letter to T. Kennard Thompson, the founder of the Engineering Society, 'up to 1889 the School was practically the Applied Science Department of University College.'

One of the activities of the UC Lit. was the holding of an annual conversazione – what we would call today an Open House – for which the various student organizations prepared lectures, experiments, and demonstrations. In the fall of 1884 Herbert J. Bowman, a third-year SPS student, suggested that the students in the Department of Engineering organize a society and participate in the conversazione. At this time the thirty-five students at SPS in regular courses and the eight special students were in three departments – Engineering, Assaying and Mining Geology, and Analytical and Applied Chemistry. Bowman's proposal received little attention until T. Kennard Thompson, a second-year student, invited *all* the second- and third-year students, some of his non-engineering friends, and Professors Galbraith and Ellis to dinner at his home on Hazelton Avenue. At the conclusion of the dinner Thompson, in replying to a toast to 'Our Host,' proposed the formation of an engineering society. The proposal was welcomed by Galbraith and accepted by all present. The meeting appointed Bruce A. Ludgate chairman of a committee to draw up a constitution, and by March 1885 the Society was in full swing, operating under the guidance of a general committee comprising Thompson as secretary, Ludgate as third-year representative, J.R. Gordon as second-year representative, and Galbraith as president.

It was characteristic of the times and of the respect in which John Galbraith was held by his students that he should be invited to be the first president. He held the position for three years, at which point it was agreed that the office should be held by a student. The first undergraduate president was H.E.T. Haultain, later distinguished professor of mining engineering.

The early constitution and practices of the new organization show that it functioned as a learning if not a learned society. The first constitution stated as the objects of the society:

a / the encouragement of original research in engineering;
b / the preservation of results of such research;
c / the dissemination of these results among its members;
d / the cultivation of a spirit of mutual assistance and co-operation among the members of the Society in the preparation for, and in the practice of, the profession of engineering;
e / the provision of an official means of communication between the student body and the Faculty Council, the university authorities, and the students of other faculties.

The first three objectives dominated the life of the new body until the first world war.

From the very beginning the primary activity of the Society was the holding of fortnightly meetings during the academic session. At these meetings undergraduates, graduates, members of staff, and invited visitors presented papers, usually of a technical nature, for discussion. Commencing in 1885 these were published annually in pamphlet form as 'Papers Read before the Engineering Society of SPS.' Representative titles included 'Asphalt Pavement' by E.F. Ball, 'Cable Railways' by W.E. Stein, and

'Review of Sanitary Science' by C.J. Marani. The pamphlets were published in quantities ranging from 400 to 1,500, and copies were exchanged with other technical societies and university libraries; this provided the nucleus for an Engineering Society Library which for many years was the only library SPS had. As we shall see, that staunch enterprise, the Engineering Stores, subsequently emerged as a spin-off from the Engineering Society Library.

But before pursuing the fascinating ramifications of the Society as publisher in applied science and engineering and supplier of goods at a price, let us be clear about who the members were and what it cost to belong. To the modern student accustomed to a substantial student affairs fee and the cumpulsory checkoff system for those fees, it may come as a shock to know that at first membership was voluntary and the annual fee was only one dollar. Membership was open to undergraduates and graduates, and for a time there were a few honorary members including Sir Cazimir Gzowski. Haultain noted in his presidential address of 1888-9 that there were 137 ordinary members – this in a year when the total undergraduate enrolment was sixty-four. The annual fee remained voluntary until, on the suggestion of Galbraith, a compulsory *library* fee of one dollar was introduced in 1893-4. This was in lieu of any other Engineering Society fee and was paid to the Society primarily to assist it in functioning as publisher. In 1908-09 the dollar fee was shown in the Calendar for the first time as an Engineering Society fee; it was increased to two dollars in 1914-15. By 1973 it had risen to seven dollars, but the role of technical publisher had long since disappeared.

Before long, the annual compendium of papers was formally renamed *The Transactions of the Engineering Society*. For a time the editor was selected by the students, but in 1897-8 it was agreed that he should be appointed by the Faculty Council. The first editor so appointed was R.W. Angus, who had edited the 1894-5 transactions as a graduate, and by this point was a teaching fellow in Electrical. Later he was professor and head of Mechanical Engineering.

During the ensuing years there developed in School a technical publishing boom. In November 1907 the annual *Transactions* were replaced by a journal called *Applied Science*, which was published monthly during the academic session with all the trappings – editorial board, subscriptions, and advertising. Some issues ran to over one hundred pages. This change coincided with the splitting of the Engineering Society into three divisions – Civil and Architecture, Electrical and Mechanical, and Chemical and Mining – each of which held technical meetings simultaneously. By this time there were 721 students; the financial problems of the Society centred around the meeting of publishing costs and the promotion of subscriptions.

Applied Science was a casualty of the first world war, the last issue appearing in 1916. In 1920-21, however, the *Transactions of the Engineering Society* reappeared. At the same time there began a companion publication, *The Transactions and Year Book of the Engineering Society,* which added a major section on student activities directed primarily at the undergraduates. By the 1940s the technical papers had become a small section of the *Transactions and Yearbook,* and by the 1950s this element had entirely disappeared. The publication had become and remains a yearbook devoted to student activities.

Even though the nature of the Society has radically changed, this early experience as learned body and technical publisher left indelible imprints on the character of School. In the co-operative activity of that period the traditional warmth and integrity of staff-student relations was established and developed. Those who wonder today whether students should be given academic credit for making speeches in the university's Governing Council, established in 1972, may be interested to know that in the 1890s the Engineering Society obtained through negotiation with the staff permission to use regular curricular time to attend technical meetings of the Society, to have marks assigned to papers presented there by students, and to have these marks considered in the determination of honour standing for the Year.

The Engineering Stores, long called the Supply Department, were closely associated in their origins with the Society's early ventures as publisher and librarian. In his annual report in October 1889, the undergraduate president stated that 'in order to afford varied reading in engineering subjects, the Society has, during the past year, fitted a small room where all books and papers, the property of the Society, are kept.' By 1891-2 the Society's librarian was making drawing paper available to fellow students at cost. By 1908 a permanent secretary had been designated to buy and sell goods through the Supplies Department. The operation eventually was separated from the library, was located in Room 19 of the sps building, and renamed the Engineering Stores. They continue to operate today in the Engineering Annex, under student management with a feminine sales staff offering, in addition to stationery, sliderules, drafting instruments, and similar items.

Few schools of engineering can boast an *esprit de corps* as strong as that which marked the School of Practical Science from its early years, and which has been regularly expressed by succeeding generations of students in the Faculty of Applied Science and Engineering through joyful renditions of the School yell:

Toike Oike, Toike Oike
Ollum Te Chollum Te Chay,
School of Science, School of Science,
Hurray, Hurray, Hurray.
We are, we are, we are the Engineers,
We can, we can, demolish forty beers ...

The original yell consisted of the first four lines. Walter H. Boyd of the Class of 1898 recalled their birth in a letter to Professor C.H.C. Wright in 1925:

It came about in this way:- A group of us, Stovel, Burnside, Carter, Piper and others thought that the School should have a catchy yell that could be used on all occasions, such as football matches, and as a triumphant yell of victory when we succeeded in stealing the bicycle racks from the Arts building (UC) and for other such stirring occasions. Each one of the group was to cease studying at night and concentrate on the composition of the yell. At a specified time, the fruits of each one's labours were duly heard and tried out. The choice was the present yell, which Piper had made up. Where he got the words 'Toike Oike' from, I do not know, but we were under the impression that he coined them for the purpose.

The lines that traditionally follow are not the particular property of School, but established themselves as part of the yell on November 25, 1905, during the procession from Rosedale Field to the King Edward Hotel following a memorable 11-9 victory by the University of Toronto rugby team over the supposedly invincible Ottawa Rough Riders. In that game F.W. (Casey) Baldwin ('06 SPS, later of aeronautical fame) had made a spectacular play in the dying minutes to win the dominion championship for the university. As was usual, the large majority at the head of the impromptu parade were Schoolmen. The addendum to the yell broke out time and time again and has never been in disuse since.

For an observer of the university scene of the 1970s, with its general lack of student joyfulness and its deadly serious sit-ins, the rivalry and frivolous capers of past generations of Schoolmen and Artsmen must form a puzzling contrast. At one time freshman students were required to wear distinctive ties at the start of term – paddy green for School, white with red dots for UC, black for Theologs, and so on. If you were a wearer of the green, you might be set upon by brigands with scissors or knives, and although your throat might accidentally be cut the coveted prize was in fact your tie – from just below the knot. If you were fleet of foot and hollered 'School,' the distress call would bring aid from all points. If you were unlucky you might be disrobed, painted, and have your clothes hung in a tree. Bags of 'tie-scalps' were prized on all sides.

Water has always been a force in engineering. It too proved to have a powerful attraction in large quantities for Schoolmen, mindful perhaps of the feats of their Roman predecessors who built the aqueducts. T.R. Loudon recounted the following incident:

On March 17, 1904 the whole of School went to the rescue of a few of its innocent second year members who had been waylaid in the Main Building (UC), and, so it was said, were being subjected to indignity. A truthful historian must perforce relate that these same innocents were accused of having used green ink to decorate noses and ears of some of their Arts companions, but of this one really cannot say, as the evidence, if any, must have been obliterated in the ensuing fray! Water was said to have flowed six inches deep out of the main door! As to the correctness of this, the writer cannot say – not having measured the stream; but certain it is that fines were eventually paid for the disappearance of about four lines of fire hose, so perhaps some budding hydraulic engineer may be able to calculate whether or not the discharge of these in the building could have produced the stream mentioned.

Rare is the graduate of School who cannot recall some such escapade. From water fights with UC, to the deposit by the Medsmen of a cow in the main drafting room, to ceremonial (but unofficial) openings by the LGMB of city halls and subways, the history of student capers at School has ranged the gamut from much good fun to disorder and near riot. If potentialities for foolishness, always present in mass behaviour, have occasionally become real, underlying them has always been an energetic and ingenious sense of tribal joy. This characteristic is well illustrated in the School's musical endeavours.

The occasion that prompted the first School song was the Royal Convocation in 1901 for the then Duke of York, later George v. This Convocation was held in the East Hall of University College. After the Duke received his honorary degree he was entertained by students representing all the faculties and colleges – the entertainment consisting mainly of college yells and songs. The School song was entitled 'A Psalm of Life at SPS' which ran to the then-popular air of 'The Dutch Companee':

Stand up! Stand up for the Science Faculty!
With Arts and the Meds they form a Trinity.
   Then shout you chaps for the SPS,
   Whose motto is meakness and peacefulness.

The first-year man when he comes up to School
Gazes with awe on a two-foot rule.
   Then shout ...

The second-year man has learned about the tap;
He sizes up the freshman with an eye to a scrap.

The third-year man'd rather fall down a mine
Than go to the depths of Constructive Design.

The fourth-year man comes back to have a fling;
He bums round the lab and he doesn't do a thing.

Now we hope this song has touched your hearts,
And you won't consign us to warmer parts.

The song was composed by A.T.C. McMaster, '01, D.H.H. Forbes, '02, and M.V. Sauer, '01, with the latter also responsible for the music. Whether His Royal Highness was conscious of the irony of the last line in the refrain is unknown.

Singing groups were formed as early as 1901 and many students, operating under such names as the School-House Four and the SPS Octet, entertained at social functions. The Toike-Oikestra was organized in 1911 by J.B. Temple, a third-year student, and many fine musicians played in it at meetings, dinners, and dances. This orchestra was disbanded during the first world war but was revived by G. Dean Maxwell in 1919.

The Toike-Oikestra was an expression of the formal interest of School-men in music; the Lady Godiva Memorial Band has demonstrated a more joyous involvement. The LGMB was organized in the fall of 1948 by A.J.P. LaPrairie, DSO, '50. Thomas Kenney, '50, was its first director. The first band had a core of eight members but grew to as many as 250 when School-men were invited to sit together at football games with any instrument they played. President Sidney Smith on occasion joined the 'band' wearing a black moustache. When he heard of the band's formation, the Lord Mayor of Coventry extended formal greetings. The name had of course been taken from that old engineering song:

Godiva was a lady who to Coventry did ride,
To show all the villagers her fine and lily white hide,
The most observant man of all, an engineer of course,
Was the only one who noticed that Godiva rode a horse ...

With their basic musical instruments supplemented by pistols, whistles, and washtubs, and sporting outlandish uniforms, the LGMB has played at so many unofficial engagements and official occasions on and off campus that no historic moment in the Metropolitan Toronto area is complete (in the members' belief) without its polyphonic renditions. As a result, for example, at the first hockey match between the University of Toronto Blues and the Soviet National Student Team in 1972, the Russians were reportedly confused by a band playing at random in the crowd. But it should also be recorded that in 1964, disguised as the Engineering Wind and Percussion Group, the LGMB, under the leadership of Don Monro, '64, won first prize for brass and reed bands (numbering less than thirty) at the Kiwanis Music Festival.

The single sound most definitively associated with School is that of a cannon. The idea may have come from the two memorial cannons on the mound in front of Hart House. *The Varsity* records that on occasion these cannons have mysteriously roared, belching smoke and flame towards Queen's Park in a modified version of the 21-gun salute which marks the opening of Parliament. In the late 1920s and early 1930s a small 'cannon' would appear at School festivities and also roar. Then it would mysteriously disappear. The authorities attempted to track down this will-o-the-wisp because it was reported to be fashioned from a crude piece of pipe mounted on a block of wood. Others believed it to be a small cannon such as that used for starting yacht races.

In 1935 at a School Auction (an annual event at which, currently, willing co-eds are 'sold' to the highest bidder to raise funds for charitable purposes) the cannon was fired on the steps of the old School building with such a charge that it shattered windows. Again it disappeared quickly.

In 1936 the Engineering Society unofficially approached a machinist working in Civil Engineering and asked if he would make a cannon. Recognizing that he was taking a considerable risk, but knowing the dangers of students' experiments with explosive charges in pipe, he decided to help. From axle stock he fashioned a 10-inch barrel with a $3/4$-inch smooth bore, and from a pillow block a base. This was accomplished in the four hours immediately preceding the School Dinner that evening. The secret was well kept.

This cannon served for thirteen years until Christmas 1949, when there appeared on the doorstep of the Engineering Society a box containing a beautiful new weapon, showing excellent workmanship. On it was engraved, 'Skule Cannon.' Santa seemed to have a close friend, a fine machinist who had been working for the Department of Civil Engineering for a long time. In 1950 the Engineering Society honoured W.H. Kubbinga with a scroll extolling his loyalty, courage, and good conduct and making him an Honorary Member in Ye Ancient and Honourable Company of Skule Cannoneers with the rank of Sergeant-Artificer.

The cannon has been popular with other than Schoolmen. In 1941, and again in 1944, students of University College managed to steal it, but each time it was retrieved. Then in 1949, during the Chariot Races, a group of hostile Meds overpowered the Cannoneers and made off with the prize. School took Bob Hetherington, president of the Medical Society, hostage and sent him to the Schoolman's Siberia (Ajax). A few days later he was exchanged for the cannon.

The roar of the cannon has come to identify a distinctive pattern of student-centred events associated with the Engineering academic year. This pattern has included the Cannonball, School Dinner, the School At-Home, School Night, the School Auction, the Chariot Races, and the Graduation Ball. School dances acquired and have retained a university-wide reputation as happy and lively occasions. By 1973 the Graduation Ball was the only formal dance still sponsored by students in the university: for hopeful graduates, wives, and sweethearts, and for the staff who are fortunate enough to attend, this night in March is still one to remember.

The first Engineering Society dinner took place on 31 January 1890 with fifty-four men present. The early dinners provided an opportunity for undergraduates, graduates, and staff to meet and mix. By 19 January 1911 the number attending had risen to six hundred. As time passed, the School Dinner became the occasion for the presentation of academic awards to undergraduates and for an address by the president of the university or some other distinguished guest. The applied mechanics of the event have included the lofting of buns and the co-ordinated clatter of cutlery dropping to the floor to test gravity.

The first School At-Home dance was held in 1911. At the second, held on 9 February 1912, in the old university gymnasium where Hart House now stands, there was suspended from the ceiling a $1/50$ scale model of the Quebec Bridge measuring 65 feet long by 6 feet high by 2 feet wide. The model, built by fourth-year Civil Engineering students with help from other years, boasted a double railroad track complete with an operating train. The socializing of the evening was rudely interrupted when the model train jumped the track. Dean Galbraith had acted as a consultant to investigate the collapse of the central span of the original bridge.

In the first decades of the century, 'theatricals' – skits presented by various departments at social events – became the rage. In the fall of 1920 the executive of the Engineering Society formally appointed a Stunt Night committee to develop this interest. The first annual 'Ngynrs in SPaSms' was presented as a review on 2 March 1921 in Massey Hall to an audience of 1,343 persons. It was directed by C.T. Carson, '23. The review consisted of thirteen different acts including 'Laboratory Lapses' and 'The Adventures of Chloreen.' Music was supplied by the Toike-Oikestra. These annual productions assumed various spellings – School Night, School Nite, Skule Nite – and prospered until they filled Hart House Theatre with Schoolmen and their friends for two- and three-day runs. But as Eric Miglin notes in his chapter on student life, the enthusiasm of undergraduates for poking fun at their own identities and that of the university rapidly waned in the sixties and the original School Night died a sociological death. For a few years, small groups of theatre-conscious Schoolmen combined forces with outside friends to produce student versions of Broadway productions such as *Stop the World, I Want to Get Off*, but these proved financially difficult and also died.

Since 1888 the election of officers and representatives has been one of the highlights in the student year of School. These elections have long symbolized that juxtaposition of serious commitment and boisterous enjoyment which is at the core of School Spirit.

The student newspaper, *Toike Oike*, made its first appearance during the Engineering Society elections of 1911 and the original issue contained statements of the policies and platforms of the candidates. The idea for the newspaper originated with J.A. Stiles, '07. During the first world war it was discontinued, but was revived in 1920 and made an official organ of the Society. Ever since, it has been published 'every now and then' but particularly at election time.

In the early days Society elections were held in the evening, and after the voting the participants would pile all the drafting tables in a corner of the first-year drafting room. This mammoth room was located on the third floor of the little red Schoolhouse. Everyone wore old clothes suitable for the celebrations, and indoor football, broomball, and chariot races ensued. In these early chariot races, each aspiring Ben Hur balanced himself on a thunder pot whose handle was threaded with tow-ropes. Fleet-footed

Schoolmen would propel the chariots around the improvised coliseum to the wild cheering of the crowd. The winners were awarded the Gerry P. Potts Trophy. In time the chariot races developed their own identity as an outdoor event at which many novel vehicles, including wheeled trash cans from City Hall, have made their appearance. When elections came to be held during the day, a half-holiday was declared for voting and festivities which often included visits to and participation in the acts at the Gayety or the Casino. The girls enjoyed the occasions more than the theatre management.

The fun of the elections had the serious purpose of attracting a dedicated group of students to lead the Society. From its unitary form in the 1890s, characterized by emphasis on collective learning and publishing, the Society developed in relation to the size and make-up of its membership. As the number of students grew, it split its technical activities first into three technical divisions and finally into clubs, each related to a specific undergraduate program or activity such as debating. In 1921 the clubs were Architectural, Chemical, Civil, Debating, Electrical and Mechanical, and Mining and Metallurgical. By 1972 Architecture and Mining had gone, Electrical and Mechanical had separated, Metallurgy had become Metallurgy and Materials Science, and Engineering Science, Geology, and Industrial had arrived. Each club elects a chairman and executive and serves the technical and social interests of its members. In several instances the clubs have become associated with student sections of Canadian and u.s. professional societies such as the Engineering Institute of Canada and the Institute of Electrical and Electronics Engineers. Through staff counsellors and invited speakers from industry, government, and the profession, the clubs have sustained in modified form the original model of staff-student relations. They also offer various dinners and smokers for the social benefit of their members.

The Debating Club deserves a special note: from the beginning it displayed the breadth of interest and initiative of Schoolmen. For example, in 1921 its chairman, G.A. Brace, then in his graduating year, was also secretary of the Inter-Collegiate Debating Union. In 1922 John Dymond and William Osbourne were debating against uc on the topic, 'Resolved that the influence of professionalism is detrimental to sport, and that professionalism should therefore be banned.' Earlier that year G.H. Rowat and T.R. Emerson of third year defeated a Wycliffe team on the question, 'Resolved that the nationalization of industry is in the best interests of industry.' In addition to such intra-university and inter-year debates, members of the club formed part of university teams in debates with McMaster, McGill, and Queen's. In its heyday, the club held meetings weekly and offered the Engineering Society Cup for the best speaker in School.

Of all the formal enterprises of the Engineering Society, the one which epitomizes the lighter side of School Spirit is the *Toike Oike*. The *Toike* appears about half a dozen times a year on no fixed dates. It is served by an elected editor and his co-opted staff. While there is extant a 1947 copy of the *Toike Oike* magazine containing technical papers, non-technical articles, and poetry, this format was clearly experimental for it did not survive. The *Toike* of history has been and remains a tabloid devoid of technical articles.

The *Toike* has regularly carried editorials about School affairs and events, news of the activities of the clubs and of the Engineering Athletic Association, commercial advertisements, and an occasional note from the dean or perhaps the president of the university. Interspersed with these serious matters are poems, jokes, cartoons, and lampoons which at their best have preserved some of the capacity of the university to laugh at itself. All the engineering sciences from thermodynamics to fluid mechanics and electrochemistry have had interpretive essays or poems written on them for the benefit of freshmen and the birds and the bees. As an example, a typical poem of 1932:

Electrochemical Eccentricities

With the cathode next the window,
And the anode next the door
Here's to Prof. Lash Miller
May he live for ever more.
And his friend Burt-Gerrans
In the coal-hole 'neath the floor
With the cathode next the window
And the anode next the door.

O, the dammed old apparatus
Will never work for us
In comes Doc Burt-Gerrans
To raise an awful fuss.
He says it's not the Demi's fault
And we begin to cuss
Because the anode's minus
Instead of being plus.

We may lose our hold on theory
Or on all Designs that be
But there's one thing we'll remember
And it's Electro-Chemistry.
If we miss the deep secrets
There's one thing sure to score
That's the cathode next the window
And the anode next the door.

If the cannon and capers, the *Toike* and the LGMB convey an aura of simple-minded good fun, this stereotype must be evaluated against the serious role of the Engineering Society as representative of the academic interests of the student body. Biting critiques of the curriculum and staff were levelled by the society long before the 'participation' battles of the university scene of the late sixties. And while Artsmen for the past several years have been concerning themselves with the theoretical principle of 'parity' between staff and students in the governance of the university, the Engineering Society has quietly negotiated a pragmatic but effective presence of students in the academic operations of the Faculty of Applied Science and Engineering.

The first formal action directed at gaining direct participation of students in the affairs of the Faculty Council was a motion by Allan Bruce, '69, on 24 October 1967 in the executive committee of the Society. His motion minced no words: it called explicitly for student representation on Council. At the next meeting of the executive his motion was adopted to direct the Society to investigate the advisability of gaining membership on the Faculty Council and some months later, in the spring of 1968, the executive agreed to do so. Still action was not precipitate. The dean was invited to attend a meeting of the executive committee for discussion of the principle, and on 8 October 1968 the executive proposed that one student representative per hundred students in the Faculty be elected to Council in the spring of each year. On 8 December 1968 the Faculty Council approved in principle the seating of elected student representatives, about twenty in number on a body of some two hundred members. Because the electoral procedures were not quickly worked out by the Society, duly elected student members first attended Faculty Council only on 12 March 1970. Interim student assessors, designated by the society, attended Council meetings from November 1969 until then, however.

During these years the university as a whole was in a turmoil of self-analysis culminating in the report of the Commission on University Government. The Faculty Council established a Special Committee on the Structure of the Faculty to work in parallel with the commission to delineate the roles of staff and students in a more formally participatory academic community. At the same time, the executive of the Engineering Society generated a series of documents that attracted wide interest among staff and students. These included 'A Preliminary Policy Position on Objectives for an Educational Environment,' September 1969 written by Art McIlwain, then president of the Society, and Wayne Richardson, and 'Students in the University,' a 45-page document issued in January 1970.

The election by the Society of students to the Faculty Council marked fundamental changes both in the Council and in the Society. In June 1972 the Board of Governors approved a new structure for the Faculty of Applied Science and Engineering in which elected students share with staff members significant responsibilities for academic development. If the new structure can exploit the thoughtful and forthright qualities of student insight that have been revealed to date, formal student participation in Faculty governance will prove refreshing and constructive.

As the Engineering Society became formally involved in the academic affairs of the Faculty, it was natural that the direction of the organization itself should be reviewed. In his year-end presidential report in the spring of 1968, John Morris, '68, remarked that the Society had emerged from being a social club to become the agent of active student government. In 1971-2 the Society developed a new constitution which provided, in addition to the conventional officers and executive committee, an Engineering Society Council empowered to act as the governing heart of the Society. This new council is composed of class representatives, the student members of Faculty Council, the representatives to the Students' Administrative Council of the university, and the executive committee of the Society.

Like the new structure of the Faculty itself, the new constitution of the Society represents a serious search for the renewal of those strong links between staff, students, and the graduates which have characterized School since 1885. The growth in scale and complexity of the Faculty and of the university has made this search difficult. But there is confidence on all sides that the Engineering Society will play a key role in the future of the Faculty, and will continue to make School one of the happier and more joyful parts of the University of Toronto.

W.W. WALKER and A.M. REID

The Engineering Alumni Association

Engineering alumni activity dates back to the first graduates of the School of Practical Science, to men who came from across Canada and the USA to sit under teachers like John Galbraith and William Hodgson Ellis. Who were the alumni? The question is not as simple to answer as it may seem, for in the early years the period of study varied as the Faculty developed, and so did the initials with which a graduate emerged. The first man to hold the three-year diploma of SPS was J.L. Morris, '81. Morris was also the first alumnus to hold the professional degree of Civil Engineer (CE), approved by the University Senate in 1884. (A graduate of SPS became eligible for this degree after he had accumulated three years of acceptable professional experience and had submitted a suitable thesis. Similar professional degrees were extended to Mechanical, Chemical, Electrical, and Mining, and were continued until 1954.) The School introduced in 1892 an optional fourth year, the completion of which established eligibility for the degree of B A SC awarded by the Senate of the University of Toronto. The first alumnus to hold both the diploma of SPS and the B A SC was T.H. Alison, '92 SPS, '93 University of Toronto. Finally, in 1909, the School (since 1900 the Faculty of Applied Science and Engineering in the University of Toronto) discontinued the three-year diploma program for students admitted that year and required all newly admitted students to study a four-year program for the B A SC.

Alumni activity began early in the life of School. Informal dinner meetings of alumni and staff were held in Toronto, Sudbury, and elsewhere. The annual dinner of the Engineering Society, initiated in 1890 when there were in all 82 graduates, was long known as the School Reunion Dinner and was designed to provide an opportunity for graduates as well as undergraduates to meet. In the calendars of sps from 1892 to 1895 are listed the officers of the Alumni Association of the School of Practical Science. Galbraith was the first president and was succeeded in 1894 by G.H. Duggan '83, then chief engineer of the Dominion Bridge Company of Montreal.

The integration of Engineering into the fabric of the university in 1906 led to a dual basis of identity for alumni, a duality usually marked by strong loyalty to both sides. Exact records of this transitional period have not been found, but we know that in 1911 J.C. Armer, '02, was president and H. Irwin, '09, secretary of an engineering alumni organization. This body consisted basically of alumni in the Toronto area, but Toike Oike Clubs, or alumni groups, existed in Montreal, Ottawa, Vancouver, and Winnipeg before the first world war. In all cases the activities were primarily social – get-togethers where men had the opportunity of continuing the fellowship they had known as undergraduates.

A reunion held in Toronto in the late fall of 1919 marks the real beginning of the present Engineering Alumni Association. Although it was supported by the local alumni body in Toronto, it was not organized by it, and to the meeting came Schoolmen from all the branch alumni organizations as well as some prominent graduates from the United States. Between a dinner on the Friday night and the Varsity football game on the Saturday afternoon, the annual meeting of the Toronto branch was scheduled in Convocation Hall, on the morning of December 13. J.L. Morris, the first graduate, was in the chair, and W.P. Dobson, '10, was secretary. A motion by R.J. Marshall, '08, seconded by C.A. Powell, and approved by the meeting, called for the creation of a centralized Engineering Alumni Association of the Universtiy of Toronto, and the appointment of a committee to prepare a constitution and by-laws. That committee included Walter J. Francis, '93, and C.E. MacDonald, '15. These two men also acted as chairman and secretary of a meeting held during the 1921 reunion at which the draft constitution was ratified.

The preamble to the constitution not only set down the aims and objectives of the association, but also noted its potential strength. Upwards of three thousand Schoolmen were scattered from coast to coast in Canada, and in many other countries. They were to be found in every industry and branch of labour, and in positions ranging from the humblest to the most exalted: if properly organized, they could become a strong power in the land. The aims of the new organization were set out as: to lend every possible assistance to the advancement of the Faculty; to perpetuate the friendship and memories of student days and maintain the loyalty and enthusiasm of the alumni for old School; to co-operate with the University of Toronto Alumni Association (which had been reorganized in 1920) in the advancement of their university's welfare; to promote increased recognition of the engineering profession and to maintain the dignity of that profession; and, finally, to develop in the membership the highest ideals of citizenship and to advance the cause of education generally and of engineering education in particular.

Since then successive councils of the Alumni Association have followed the course charted by the original organizers. As with all constitutions, the 1921 document has from time to time had to be amended in minor details – in 1936, 1945, 1948, and 1955 – and in 1960 a major revision was prepared under the chairmanship of John Fox, '27. But with all the changes that have taken place, the underlying philosophy of the original still holds firm, its aims and objects an ever-present challenge for each new executive.

The day-to-day business of the Association is carried on by a Council composed of seven elected officers, ten elected councillors, and certain *ex-officio* members. The officers are the honorary president, the president, three vice-presidents, a secretary, and treasurer; all are normally residents of Metropolitan Toronto or its close environs except for the third vice-president, who must live more than thirty miles from Metropolitan Toronto and is considered the out-of-town representative on council. The *ex-officio* members include the immediate past president; Engineering alumni sitting on the university's governing body; the president of the fourth year; the chairman of any committee appointed by the council or by the association at its annual meeting; and the members of the advisory board. The latter is an honorary body consisting of the president of the university, all past presidents of the Association, and others who may be elected by the council from time to time in recognition of their genuine interest in the Association's activities. The officers and other elected councillors, as might be expected, provide the core of active workers, but the *ex-officio* members are useful as advisers. The calibre of councillors over the years has been outstanding, and credit must be given to the nominating committees who have found so many dedicated men. It is largely because of their efforts that the Engineering Alumni Association is recognized as one of the strongest alumni groups on the campus. The following have served as president of the association:

1921-24	W.J. Francis	1927-30	J.M.R. Fairbairn
1924-27	A.E.F. Bunnell	1930-33	C.E. MacDonald

1933-36	W.D. Black	1956-58	J.R. White
1936-39	A.R. Robertson	1958-60	W.H. Palm
1939-42	H.E. Wingfield	1960-62	W.I.M. Turner
1942-45	M.B. Hastings	1962-64	J.H. Fox
1945-48	O. Holden	1964-66	W.J. MacNeill
1948-49	W.A. Osbourne	1966-68	R.F. Moore
1949-50	A.H. Frampton	1968-70	J.W. Powlesland
1950-52	W.R. Carruthers	1970-72	F.T. Gerson
1952-54	M.C. Stafford	1972-	J.G. Cowan
1954-56	C.A. Morrison		

Let us turn now from the origin and organization of the Engineering Alumni Association to its impact on the individual Schoolman who reads this chapter. He may find it affects him on three levels.

First, as a member of the Association, he may support it through his contributions, his presence at reunions, and his suggestions for future development. Second, as a member of a specific graduating year, he will have bonds he may wish to maintain with others who shared the same experiences in lecture halls and labs, and with whom he may still work in the outside world. And third, as an individual alumnus, he represents his faculty and university in the community, and will be able to contribute there through the training he received at School and the contacts he made there with classmates and others on the campus.

In the following pages some effort will be made to cover these three levels of alumni membership – in the association as a whole, in the year, and in the community.

The social activities that are so often seen as the chief concern of an organized alumni body have always received due attention from the engineers. The first of a series of Triennial Reunions that continues to this day was held fifty-two years ago. The decision to hold reunions every three years was doubtless a compromise: annual events were impractical to attempt, and five years was too long an interval. In the early days the reunions were held on campus, but as the need for more accommodation developed the Royal York Hotel became the focal point for many years. The format of these two-day affairs was relatively fixed – a dinner dance (sometimes formal, sometimes not) on Friday, business meetings on Saturday morning, class luncheons on both days, a football game on Saturday afternoon, and a stag dinner on Saturday night.

The mid-sixties saw a significant change in the pattern. The reunions returned to the campus, specifically to Hart House, where engineers for the first time could consume their 'forty beers' in academically Gothic halls. (The refreshment policies of the university had for years been a real obstacle to the use of the campus for reunions.) The 1966 Triennial is also remembered as the one that honoured R.R. McLaughlin, '22, on his retirement as dean of the Faculty, and saw the incoming dean, James Ham, '43, take a wrecking hammer and strike the first blow in the razing of the old School of Practical Science building that had stood at the southeast corner of the front campus since 1878.

In 1965 a new and annual Spring Reunion Dinner was inaugurated to honour those who had graduated twenty-five, forty, fifty, and sixty years before. These June dinners have grown quickly in popularity and attendance, and through the concentration on four graduating years have done much, systematically and effectively, to build alumni support. A highlight of these dinners, which are held in New College, has been the appearance of the Lady Godiva Memorial Band. The members of this unlikely School concession to the arts mask their musical prowess in antics and costumes that bring listeners to their feet in spontaneous appreciation of the raucous good humour. At the end of their concert, as at the end of all reunions, comes a standing 'Toike Oike,' delivered with gusto and nostalgia for the flippant ditty that is the vocal bond of all good Schoolmen.

In the early years, a loud 'Toike Oike' was almost all that was needed to initiate an engineering get-together. But as more men graduated each year and spread across Canada and throughout the world, it became increasingly difficult to maintain the friendships developed in undergraduate days. The need for improved communication became apparent. Thus evolved the association's first newsletter, the *Alumni Toike Oike,* published 'every now and then' but a welcome letter from home to many who received it on the frontiers of a developing Canada. It answered the 'I wonder what Charley's doing?' type of question, keeping alumni in touch with the activities and progress of their fellows.

In order to avoid confusion with the undergraduate newspaper, also called *Toike Oike,* the publication was renamed *Engineering Alumni News* in 1954. Since then it has been published by the Alumni Council, generally four times a year. It makes no pretence to be a professional piece of work (although one of its more experienced editors once leaned on the old Toronto Star building); but through its circulation to more than sixteen thousand graduates it serves as a vehicle of publicity for many Association activities. It trumpets the approach of each reunion and proclaims the winners of alumni scholarships, awards, and medals. Over the years it has also brought to alumni attention a number of special events not directly associated with the regular activities of the Association.

A good example is the way it rallied hundreds of engineers in a final salute to the little red Schoolhouse. When it was first found that the old SPS building stood in the path of progress and would be scrapped to make way for the new Medical Sciences Building, it appeared that the only carillon to be rung for its passing would be the thud of the wrecker's hammer. The high Victorian edifice which had sheltered thousands of engineers and nurtured them through their tender years of learning was about to succumb to age and obsolescence, alone and forgotten.

'Gentlemen,' the *News* asked in February 1966, 'is this the way to leave an old friend? Is this repayment for the fond memories these old red walls have provided us? ... All we ask is that School go to its final resting place knowing it has not been forgotten, that its memory is still cherished by thousands, that its eighty-eight years of service since 1878 are recalled with respect and gratitude.'

Who would have believed that a bunch of hardbaked engineers would respond to this maudlin appeal? But respond they did. The late Les Vardon, chairman of the council's *ad hoc* brick committee, was swamped with letters from alumni anxious to buy one or more of the red bricks that had made up the Schoolhouse. One graduate in Connecticut replied immediately asking for a brick and offering up to $10 for it. The resulting program carried bits and pieces of the old building around the world. Pieces of brick were embedded in lucite for paperweights, others were dolled up as pseudo-functional pen holders, and hundreds of plain old red bricks were sent out unadorned – as plain old red bricks. Bannisters were made into gavels for the presidents of graduating classes. Worn stair treads, transformed into bookends emblazoned with the School crest, have become collectors' items. So the final resting place of the Schoolhouse was not a junkyard, but close to the men who had sung its fame for decades.

Three formal reminders of it remain on the campus. The first is a handsome plaque, presented by the Engineering Alumni Association, that adorns the west entrance of the Medical Sciences Building, commemorating the location of the old School – surely, to oldtimers, an unexpected wedding with that old rival, Meds. The second is the lintel stone from the old north doorway that bears the name, School of Practical Science. This stone was placed in a wall of the quadrangle of the Galbraith Building by the Class of 1923. The third is an oil painting of the School building by Tom Roberts, commissioned by the Association. Reproductions of it were made available to alumni who contributed to the Varsity Fund, and prompted a

40 per cent increase in donations from engineers. The original now hangs in the Faculty Council chamber in the Galbraith Building, overseeing present deliberations with a reminder of the past.

The minutes of the Association's general and executive meetings and the alumni newsletter provide a capsule history of the financial side of the organization, but any reader who attempted to follow through such a history might speedily conclude that he was caught in a revolving door, for the Engineering Alumni Association's status with the University of Toronto Alumni Association has fluctuated from full constituency to complete divorce and back again. Membership has also fluctuated. The treasurer's report for 1933 showed that the number of members had dropped from 1,062 in 1930 to 631 – the reason probably being the depression. The annual fee then was $3, split equally between the Association, the newsletter, and the University of Toronto Alumni Federation. Numbers were soon restored to earlier levels, but did not show any significant increase until the association launched its Engineering Committee Fund in 1948.

In 1955, the Engineers led the way in a re-organization of alumni affairs on a university-wide basis by supporting the newly born Alumni Fund and agreeing that appeals to graduates should be consolidated in a single plea. Contributions, except for $2 to cover administrative costs, were at this point divided between the Alumni Fund and the Engineering Alumni Association. An editorial in the May 1956 issue of the *Engineering Alumni News* reported that the experiment had proved 'a marked success.' Engineers had in the first year contributed almost three times as much to the Alumni Fund as to any previous specific appeal from the Engineering Alumni Association.

In 1959, the revitalized alumni body threw its effort behind the National Fund appeal, run by the university to gain capital funds to meet the building needs of a huge new student generation. While the man singled out would want to share the credit with Bill Palm, '33, and others, the council's 1960 minutes record appreciation to Bill Turner, '25, for 'thorough and inspiring leadership' which resulted in 2,651 engineers pledging $495,275 in the campaign. The Association suspended its own annual drive for funds during these years; in return, the university underwrote the Association's annual budget.

The National Fund was followed by the Varsity Fund, an annual appeal for contributions to provide the university with 'the margin of excellence,' as President Claude Bissell described it, to maintain and enhance Toronto's standing and to finance innovation. Bill Palm was instrumental in converting the enthusiasm generated by the National Fund to this new venture. One of the techniques used was a telephoning 'bee' to graduates in the Metropolitan Toronto area to garner donations. The first telethon in 1961 raised close to $25,000 for the university and the Association from engineers in Metro alone. The idea has caught on, and has spread to other cities. In 1971, 4,079 engineers contributed $96,111 as part of a university-wide telephone campaign. It is clear that engineers will continue to assist the University of Toronto financially in providing the excellence they expect of their alma mater. The Association for its part is committed to its own program of financial aid to students; to maintaining the bond between Faculty, university, and graduates; and to support of the Varsity Fund.

One of the original aims and objectives of the Association, it will be remembered, was to promote increased recognition of the engineering profession. It occurred to one alumnus, A.M. (Tony) Reid, '23, that one way to do this was to publicly honour outstanding achievement by graduates in the field of engineering. His proposal was placed before the council and approved at the ninth general meeting of the Association in 1936. Thus was born the Engineering Alumni Medal.

The medal itself was designed by a distinguished Canadian sculptor, Emmanuel Hahn. The dies were cut at the Royal Mint in Britain, and the medals were struck at the Mint in Ottawa. The design is unusual in two respects – its symbolism and its simplicity. The face carries a stark representation of Archimedes' statement, 'Give me a place to stand and a lever long enough, and I will move the earth,' Emmanual Hahn captured this with a curve to represent the earth, a lever, a fulcrum, the Greek phrase *dos pou sto* ('Give place stand'), and the name, Archimedes. On the reverse is the University of Toronto oak tree, the name of the university, and in large capitals: ENGINEERING ALUMNI. FOR ACHIEVEMENT.

At least nine months before each Triennial Reunion, the Alumni Council appoints a nominating committee for the medal, and a selection committee. The award is made by the president during the reunion, following the reading of a citation. Soon after the inception of this honour, it was decided that when two deserving recipients were identified, two medals could be awarded. On one occasion three men had been so intimately involved in a special project that a further exception was made and all three received medals. The presentation ceremony has become one of the highlights of each reunion. The medal winners to date have been:

1939   C.R. Young and Arthur S. Runciman
1942   W.P. Dobson and W.E. Phillips

1945 W.G. Swan and H.G. Thompson
1948 H.R. Banks and Winnett Boyd
1951 J.H. Parkin and J.R. White
1954 Eldon L. Brown and M.V. Sauer
1957 G.B. Langford
1960 Otto Holden and Charles W. West
1963 J.B. Challies and R.A. Forward
1966 James A. Chamberlin and Beverley S. Shenstone
1969 Fraser W. Bruce, John T. Dyment, and William S. Kirkpatrick

This is perhaps a good point at which to refer to another ceremony with special meaning to every graduate – the Ritual of the Calling of an Engineer. While entirely under the administration of the Wardens of the Iron Ring in Toronto, in co-operation with the Corporation of the Seven Wardens in Montreal, and independent of any university or professsional body, or indeed of the Engineering Alumni Association, nevertheless it has proved an important bond of professional fellowship across Canada. The iron ring, presented during the ceremony and worn on the little finger of the working hand, identifies an engineer who has taken part in the ritual. The idea for this unique Canadian rite stemmed from the late Professor H.E.T. Haultain, a graduate of 1889. As a result of a letter from him, Rudyard Kipling wrote the ritual in the form that has been used, unchanged, since 1925. It was a group of Toronto alumni, all members of the Engineering Alumni Association council, who formed Camp 1 and put on the first ceremony for the graduating class that year.

From the beginning, the Alumni Association has been concerned with service to those outside its own ranks – with helping future and present undergraduates, and with promoting the welfare of School as an educational institution. It has long had an active engineering education committee. In 1939 that committee, under the leadership of H.E. (Pat) Wingfield, '23, created a counselling group of alumni and produced a booklet to assist the members of that group in the vocational guidance of young Ontarians considering registration in Engineering at Toronto. The objective was to improve continually the quality of undergraduates entering the Faculty. Alumni were recruited in sufficient numbers so that one could be assigned to nearly every secondary school in the province which had courses leading to engineering. The booklet was brought up to date in 1948 and again in 1950.

During the period extending from 1950 well into the 1960s, there was a natural tendency for high school students with ability in mathematics and the sciences to seek entrance to SPS. A minimum of expert guidance was needed to help them find their way. The dramatic changes in both secondary and postsecondary education in the 1960s and early 1970s, by contrast, placed great demands upon all those concerned with career counselling, and particularly upon those concerned with the guidance of prospective engineers. During this period, the Faculty accepted increased responsibility in this activity, marked by the appointment in 1970 of Professor J.S. Hewitt to the position of secondary school liaison officer. At this writing, steps are being taken to renew alumni involvement in the guiding of young Canadians into modern engineering and the SPS tradition.

Direct financial assistance to students by the Association was begun in 1959. The counselling service was supplemented by a bursary program which awarded about $7,500 annually to between twenty and thirty students who had demonstrated financial need as well as good academic standing, leadership, and character. The counselling group was used to interview applicants and report to the education committee. In addition, a revolving loan fund, built up by contributions from individual graduating classes, was made available to undergraduates requiring financial assistance. This fund rose through donations to some $16,000; it is a tribute to Schoolmen that no bad debts were ever incurred.

When the Ontario government began a large-scale student award program in the mid-sixties, the Alumni Council recognized that it should change the format of its own educational assistance. Under the government scheme of loans and grants (intended to ensure that no youngster need be deprived of a university education for lack of money alone), any other financial assistance (such as the Engineering loans and bursaries) limited the amount of financial support available to a student from the province. As a result, in 1968 the bursary fund was placed in the hands of the Faculty secretary to provide a discretionary fund to support undergraduates who find themselves in financial difficulties during the academic year. The loan fund also became inactive during the late sixties, and was replaced by a series of seven annual $1,000 entrance scholarships created to attract top students to the Faculty. The scholarship program has been financed partly by gradual depletion of the loan fund, partly with money from the Varsity Fund.

As part of this continuing effort in the area of student support, the Engineering Alumni Association in 1965 established the Stewart Wilson Award, named in tribute to the former secretary and assistant dean of the Faculty (and graduate of 1921), who is remembered by countless Schoolmen as a friend and counsellor. The award, which has a value in excess of $1,000, provides accommodation in a room furnished by the Association in the men's residence of New College, – a college which Wilson helped get started as assistant to its principal after he retired from Engineering. The room was officially inaugurated at the spring reunion in June 1965. The winner of this award must be a second-year Engineering student and a member of New College, and must have exhibited in his first year academic skill plus keen involvement in extracurricular activities. Selection is made by the engineering education committee.

Another important facet of Association activity is represented by the undergraduate relations committee. This body has for its objective the development of stronger ties between undergraduates and graduates through the encouragement of worthwhile activities within the Faculty. This goodwill has been demonstrated in various ways. The alumni financed the relocation and refurnishing of the Engineering Stores when it was necessary to move from the old location in the Schoolhouse. They have helped with the purchase of instruments and contributed towards travelling expenses of the Lady Godiva Memorial Band. They have also assisted students travelling to inter-university conferences. Currently, the Association's council is following with interest an undergraduate proposal for a unified Engineering Activities Centre on campus. Less concretely, this committee also endeavours to assist graduating years to choose their permanent executives wisely from among members who are likely to remain in the Toronto area so as to ensure a nucleus for future alumni activity.

Among the various graduating classes of Engineering, some special combination of circumstances seems to operate to promote unusual spirit and activity in some years, and so to bring these classes into the limelight. Perhaps they give unusual support to the Engineering Alumni Association: 1925, to cite an outstanding example, has supplied three presidents to that body. Or they may develop particular projects, either related to, or independent of, the Association and the Faculty. As previously noted, the Class of 1923, which still holds monthly dinners in Hart House throughout the winter, arranged for the preservation of the lintel stone from the north entrance of the old School building when the wreckers approached, and saw it installed appropriately in the Galbraith Building. The same class has contributed $1,000 to the university, to be held with accrued interest until the one hundredth anniversary of its graduation in 2023, at which time the money is to be used to support a graduate student carrying out research for a thesis based on the extensive set of records that has been accumulated by the class since 1923 and now rests in the University Archives.

Other examples come to mind readily. The Class of 1927 is providing a significant centennial addition to the Engineering Library. The Class of 1945 arranged for the payment of tuition fees for an overseas student. The Class of 1935 established the Second Mile Award and thus has sent some twenty graduates out into the world with an appreciation of the value of a helping hand for fellow men. Many more projects could be listed. The important lesson is that an active class organization continues through a lifetime, and for the benefit of others, the fellowship developed during undergraduate years.

Now we come to the individual alumnus, who represents the grass roots – the basic element – of both Association and class. In age he varies from the most recent graduate to the one who hopes to get to the next reunion even if it kills him. His attitude naturally will be affected by his years and by the climate of the time in which he finds himself. This volume is in great part devoted to the story of the past fifty years. Those who have graduated in the past decade or so – and they constitute a large proportion of the total – may be more concerned with establishing their own careers and building a family than in trying to imagine what it was like when the School Psalm was written. Most alumni have developed a strong feeling of belonging to a group with special traditions – they are Schoolmen. From this basis of loyalty to School many have gone on to recognize that as graduates they are members of a university that is going through trying times, and may be wondering what responsibilities they have under the circumstances.

Fortunately a careful analysis of the situation has been carried out by a group of men and women (including two engineers) and has been published under the title, *Alumni in the University Community,* the report of the President's Long Range Planning Committee on Alumni Affairs. An abridged version was published in the *University of Toronto News* of February 1972. Even with excision it is a long document, and the reader may have filed it away for 'future reference.' The time needed to read it may not yet have been found, but what is his response to a statement like this? 'Most [alumni] associations are still oriented to programs that were the norm several decades ago, emphasizing reunions, cocktail parties, and so on. Recently alumni seem more inclined to respond to intellectual opportunities.'

The key word here seems to be *respond*. What is necessary for such response? To begin with, the individual alumnus must know what opportunities exist. More efforts are being made to provide accurate information about what is happening at the university through the *Engineering Alumni*

News and the *University of Toronto News*. But special responsibility rests on the 'authorities' (alumni and university staff) to define goals and improve the means of communication. The Faculty has already responded by making provision for fifteen alumni members, designated by the association, to serve on the Faculty Council and its major committees.

Every step must be taken to encourage the individual alumnus to involve himself in the ongoing life of the Faculty and the university at various levels, and so to make his own contribution to the community. Who is to do this? It may be argued by those outside the Metropolitan Toronto area that it can be left to those on the spot in Toronto. Others may say they are too busy, that they will forward an annual cheque to the Varsity Fund but, as to other matters, they will leave those to 'George' – in this case the Council of the Engineering Alumni Association. And to a great extent the council is actively performing such a role for all engineering alumni within the Faculty and as one of the key constituents of the University of Toronto Alumni Association.

Nevertheless, much rests – and has always rested – with the individual to represent and interpret the university and its influence in his community. Through their particular kind of training, Schoolmen may find themselves in positions of leadership. That they have performed such functions well in the past – as civic leaders, chairmen of various bodies, innovators, and policy consultants – is made clear in chapter 10. But now something more may be required. In an address upon receiving the degree of Doctor of Engineering at Carleton University, Professor Bernard Etkin, '41, future dean of the Faculty, asked: 'What responsibility falls on you and me ... if we are to succeed in controlling "the monsters of technology"?' He replied:

> On the personal level, we need to broaden our criteria beyond the narrow ones of the Kipling Obligation. Let me read you part of a proposal for a Hippocratic Oath for Applied Scientists proposed by Professor Thring, of the University of London. 'I vow to strive to apply my professional skills only to projects which, after conscientious examination, I believe to contribute to the goal of co-existence of all human beings in peace, human dignity and self-fulfilment.'

There is some indication that this extension of engineering ethics is of growing concern to the younger element in the profession. This is discussed elsewhere in this book by Eric Miglin. (The fact that Mr Miglin was elected president of the Students' Administrative Council for 1972-3 may be taken as a happy indication that engineers will continue to be cast in roles of leadership, even as darts are thrown at technocrats and technology.

His election by a campus-wide vote is also reassuring evidence that – despite all the newspaper reports of student disturbances – the majority of today's undergraduates still have a sober and serious attitude towards their university life.)

If the alumnus is to perform such an expanded role, he will have to take the opportunity to play a greater part in the educational and recreational world of the campus. The application may be most evident for younger graduates, but even the older ones must recognize that education is a continuing process and that we owe it to ourselves to develop our potential so as to contribute effectively to society even as the years hurry on. Nor need the process end with retirement from business or profession. The 'second career' concept so well presented by Dr Wilder Penfield is a challenge that has been accepted by many engineers, to their own satisfaction and the good of the community.

The pages of this chapter and of the *Engineering Alumni News* record a succession of projects which the Engineering Alumni Association has undertaken, for the most part in close and harmonious co-operation with the Faculty. Experience shows that the best of these programs are those which call upon the members to *act* in addition to asking them to think and/or pay. If the call to action is well conceived and orchestrated, the implementation usually is successful and the response encouraging.

The evolution of the University of Toronto Act, 1971, which has resulted in the creation of a new Governing Council, was monitored by, and one might hope influenced by, the work of an Engineering alumni task force which acted as liaison with the full Association. Engineers have always been proud members of their university. They have been consistent in their support, not only of their own Faculty, but of the academic thrust of the entire university. That was the spirit which prompted the Engineering Alumni Association to write to the president-designate, Dr John Evans, on the day his appointment was announced:

> As your fellow alumni, we have some inkling of the opportunities, the joys and the trials awaiting you ...
>
> Please count us among your staunch allies whenever you have problems to solve, but above all, please rely on our enthusiastic support for any project which will add to the health, strength and accomplishments of the University.

These sentiments were, be it remembered, addressed to a distinguished alumnus of the Faculty of Medicine!

In the future Engineering alumni must prepare themselves for more direct involvement in the affairs of their Faculty and of their campus. They have long been well represented on the Senate and on the Board of Governors of the University. But until last year the presence of members of the Alumni Association on these bodies was a tribute to their individual competence and achievements rather than to their membership in the Association *per se*. The new Governing Council of the university includes eight members 'of the Alumni elected from among the Alumni,' and while these are not chosen directly by one alumni association they are intended to represent the graduates.

Why do so many able and distinguished men and women devote time and effort to the Engineering Alumni Association? In general, because they want to share in the task of making the University of Toronto the best possible university, and its Faculty of Applied Science and Engineering the finest possible engineering school. In the pursuit of that objective, they find the satisfaction and enjoyment and good fellowship referred to at the start of this chapter.

The association can face the future with a great deal of confidence in its members, its resources, and its traditions. It knows the Faculty and the University of Toronto as places where excellence will always be nurtured, where leaders will be spawned, where the boundaries of knowledge will be exploded, expanded, and, one hopes, evaluated and integrated into individual lives for the public benefit, and it will work for the continued prosperity of both institutions.

The Association is moving to improve further the standard of communication with all alumni. Its work is a reminder that among their peers graduates can rediscover the roots of their professional competence and an awareness of what the university has given them – not only the means to marshal new technologies, but also the ability to understand them and their impact in life and values.

In Ontario there is some suggestion that the professional, technical, and learned societies have not succeeded in appealing to these aims among engineers. There is also evidence that academic excellence may be impaired by the bureaucratic machinery needed to operate large institutions of learning. These make cogent reasons why the University of Toronto, and especially the Faculty of Applied Science and Engineering, should once again become the focus of what is best in the thoughtful application of professional excellence to daily life.

The twenties

Before trying to answer the question 'How did it feel to be a student in the Faculty of Applied Science in the twenties?' it would be well to consider the scene in which the undergrads of those far-off days found themselves. How different from the situation today, whether we consider the physical plant or the prevailing atmosphere.

First let us look at the place as it was. The campus was much as it had been for years. The Main Building, as University College was usually called, presided calmly over the scene. It contained some of the administrative offices. The round tower at the west end was called the Senate Building. The little building to the east, which had originally been an observatory, still seemed open to the skies. 'Old School' held its place south of the campus, supported by the Mining Building on College Street. Our neighbours were the Medical Building to the east and the Physics Building and Convocation Hall to the west. Further afield were buildings inhabited by Theologs, the Methodists at Victoria on the northeast corner of Queen's Park Crescent, the Presbyterians at Knox on the Spadina Crescent, Anglicans at Wycliffe, at its present location, and Old Trinity, still located on Queen Street West. The Roman Catholics at St Michael's occupied a large area east of Queen's Park but were more or less out of sight. Hart House was new, released from wartime use for the first time in the fall of 1919, but the Soldiers' Tower had not yet appeared. St George Street was noted for the number of fraternities that proudly displayed their Greek letters. Baldwin House, later renamed Cumberland and turned into the home of the International Student Centre, a one-time stately residence at the northeast corner of St George and College, had not yet been acquired by the university. Parking was no problem for there were few cars on the campus. It was indeed, to cite the Engineering song, a scene of 'meekness and peacefulness.'

More difficult is the task of describing the climate or atmosphere. Dr Claude Bissell, speaking at Macdonald College, Montreal, in April 1971, described the institutional transformation of the University of Toronto during his thirteen years as president as a change from 'a quiet place for contemplation and inspiration' to 'a giant complex multiversity.' Yet his years as president spanned only the latter portion of the half-century we are asked to recall. In the 1920s the world was still trying to recover from a war in which Canada had played a gallant part, and which had left its mark on all institutions, including universities, and on individuals, young and old alike. Men came back from service overseas in many cases to join the unemployed; others returned to resume or commence their university studies. Owing to their experiences and their added years, these ex-soldiers tended to dominate the scene. A statement compiled in the Faculty office at the time recorded the division shown in table 1 among those who wrote their examinations in the spring of 1919.

TABLE 1

	Total	Ex-soldiers	Non-soldiers
First year	376	173	203
Second year	164	82	82
Third year	139	79	60
Fourth year	93	60	33
	772	394	378

Ex-soldiers made up slightly more than 50 per cent of the whole. The average age of the first year that October was 21.6 years, of the second 22.2, of the third, 24, and of the fourth, 25.

Why did students in those days choose a particular department? Dean C.H. Mitchell noted in one of his annual reports what appeared to be a swing towards the industrial branches of the profession. The registration in 1920-1 was: Electrical, 216; Mechanical, 159; Civil, 154; Chemical, 146; Mining, 66; Metallurgy, 18; Architecture, 33; Analytical Chemistry, 15 – total of 807 in all years. Civil Engineering may have attracted those who had had some experience in war or elsewhere in construction or organization; it appealed to others as a general course. Mining may have attracted the more adventurous. It could be argued that the Miners and Civils were more the outdoor type and the Electricals and Chemicals more the indoor lab type, with the Mechanicals falling in between. In those days the Architects occupied quarters in the old red Schoolhouse. They obtained the same degree of B A SC on graduation but kept pretty much to themselves and probably looked down on the uncultured and rough lads in School proper. The Chemicals looked to be a younger lot on the average and stuck together very definitely. Their war-cry, grounded in the then-current laxatives, was often heard: 'Nujol, Cascarets, A B S and C, Chemicals, Chemicals, Chemicals 2T3.' It came as a challenge to less vocal departments. The E & M group tended to be a silent majority.

The Civils and Miners used to come together for a six-week summer course in surveying at the Gull Lake Camp, which the Faculty established in the Haliburton area in 1920. It was a happy and healthy experience in which water and other sports played a part in keen, good-natured competition. One year, despite being outnumbered, the Miners tied at the final event of the season – jumping or diving from the top of a lofty tower. Credit was given for each man who made the jump from the highest point. Finally one Miner who had never done anything of the kind was persuaded to sacrifice his fears to the cause. He climbed up with a friend and then, hand in hand, they plunged down to the applause of all. Another win for the Miners.

The new undergrads in the early twenties quickly recognized the influence of a number of personalities whose names deserve still to be remembered. Sir Robert Falconer has been described as the last of the great Canadian university presidents. He was respected for his unassuming dignity and his scholarly and kindly approach. He despised wealth for wealth's sake, and used to point as an example of waste to a rich man chewing a cigar in the lobby of some grand hotel, bored and with nothing to do. The dean, Brig-Gen Mitchell, had collected a remarkable number of awards in his wartime career and had brought home many souvenirs of Europe. Among them were the fragments of stained glass from the battlefields of Flanders which were incorporated in the windows of Hart House chapel, and an enormous eighteen-inch brass shell case – a memento of the Italian campaign – which he presented to the Class of 1923 at their graduation luncheon. He combined public duties such as the presidency of the Board of Trade with his deanship until his retirement in 1941.

Peter Gillespie was a popular professor who threw himself into his lectures with a vast amount of energy, sometimes to the point of forgetting practicality. The story is told, doubtless with variations, of how, with

The first graduate of the School of Practical Science, James L. Morris of the Class of '81 – engineer, civil servant, author, and politician.

One of School's most famous graduates: pioneer aviator
J.A.D. McCurdy, '07, at the controls of the *Silver Dart*,
in which he made the first flight over British territory at
Baddeck, Nova Scotia, on 23 February 1909.
Opposite: In 1906, as part of a now-forgotten prank,
his class presented Professor Graham with a turkey. In
the centre picture, Dean John Galbraith (furthest right
of the three central figures) surveys the field after a
School-Meds scrap about the same time. And yes, even
in those days the undergraduates were surveying the
front campus.

This fracas is alleged to be the School initiation of 1914.

The Engineering Stores in Room S-19 of the old Schoolhouse.

A Schoolhouse office of nearly half a century ago.
Miss Rose Cave was for many years
secretary to Professor K.B. Jackson.

When Architecture was a part of SPS,
Professor C.H.C. Wright used this office
as its head.

The little red Schoolhouse in 1927.

Members of the Faculty, with some associates, at the
Gull Lake Camp in 1927. Front row: A.D. LePan,
W.M. Treadgold, Dean C.H. Mitchell, L.B. Stewart,
C.H.C. Wright. Second row: E.A. Smith, G.R.
Anderson, J. Roy Cockburn, F.C. Dyer. Third row:
D. Maxwell, J.W. Melson, E.S. Moore, J.W. Bain, S.R.
Crerar. Fourth row: E.G.R. Ardagh, K.B. Jackson,
W.B. Dunbar, three unidentified members of the party,
and, at far right partially hidden by the post, H.E.T.
Haultain.
Opposite: C.R. Young, the Faculty's first historian, and
dean from 1941 to 1949.

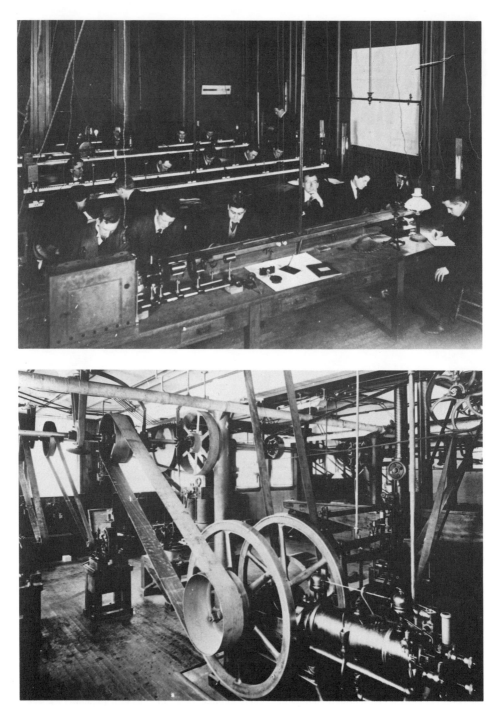

An optical lab in operation in 1909, and a gas-driven engine and dynamo about the turn of the century.

School's first wind tunnel for aeronautical studies, built by J.H. Parkin.
Below: electrical testing lab.

Scenes from the Gull Lake Survey Camp:
a composite album of snapshots taken during
the twenties and thirties.

A brief survey of student views of student life in a decade punctuated by war. Clockwise from bottom left: in the mid-thirties, an unfortunate clambers for his trousers; bookwork has always been the undergraduate constant, whether at home with blueprints or in the old Civil-Electrical Library; an early model of the School Cannon, *circa* 1938; training for real fire in the COTC after 1939; following the final surrender, hijinx returned as a new Engineering campus opened at Ajax.

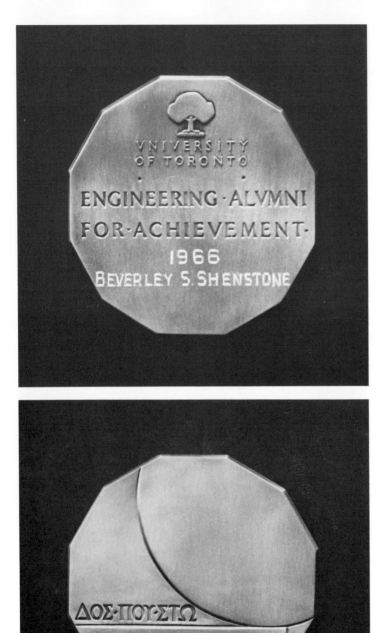

The Engineering Alumni Medal for outstanding professional achievement has been awarded to twenty-two men since its inception in 1939.

sliderule in hand, he once concluded a calculation of some length: 'Two times two' (consulting his sliderule) 'Three-point-nine – call it four.' Of his sincere interest in his students, there was no doubt. Following his death in May 1929 the dean noted: 'His place cannot well be filled as he was a unique teacher, an eminent civil engineer of wide knowledge, and a man of charming personality.'

C.R. Young taught a fundamental course on strength of materials. His long-term aim was to broaden the engineering course so that it would provide an education equal to that of any other faculty and not merely technical training. He hoped that the disciplined mind and the moral energy of the engineer would bring a powerful influence to bear on the solution of Canadian problems. 'C.R.' later became head of the Civil Engineering department and then dean of the Faculty. He held many outside offices, including that of president of the Engineering Institute of Canada.

We always felt we were learning something from T.R. (Tommy) Loudon. Never hurried, always clear and direct in his explanations and diagrams, Tommy built for himself a reputation that did much to bind the teaching staff and students together, and interpreted for the latter how a subject should be presented. He had some advantages, both in his long association with sport and in his service overseas, but the fundamental reason for the regard in which he was held was that he could see the students' point-of-view.

J. Roy Cockburn was a tall, friendly, sandy-haired man, completely ambidextrous, with a ready smile and a large pair of wooden compasses, who described weird and wonderful diagrams on the blackboard. We didn't skip many of his lectures even if we did have his little book. He had done his bit in the war: using his mathematical training, he had developed a method for locating enemy guns from the sound received at two registered points. He was also an accomplished figure skater.

The Chemicals will always remember Professor James Watson Bain as a quiet, kindly gentleman to whom students went for guidance, whose door was always open to anyone in difficulty. Not only the students from his own course, but many others felt he was on their side and understood their troubles. Long after his retirement he corresponded with former students and exchanged Christmas cards. His tenure of office as head of his department is marked by an oil painting which hangs in the Wallberg Building.

H.E.T. Haultain's students, on the other hand, chanted:

We are miners seeking riches,
We are Haultain's sons of bitches.

Professor Haultain came to SPS from the hurly-burly of the B.C. mining camps. This lent a certain enjoyable saltiness to his lectures. It also gave him an appreciation of the need among engineers for a strict sense of ethics, which he emphasized at every opportunity. It was Haultain who sponsored the adoption of the Kipling Ritual and the 'Iron Ring' ceremony.

These men and others had an influence far beyond their lectures. They contributed to that 'something' that gives graduates, men and women alike, wisdom that cannot be extracted from books alone.

Many graduates also will remember the genial, friendly, and helpful figure of Stewart Wilson. Stew had graduated in Architecture in 1921, was appointed instructor in Engineering Drawing in 1923, secretary of the Faculty in 1927, and assistant dean in 1941. After a short retirement, he became assistant to the principal of New College in 1962. He was a power behind the scenes for years and a great influence for good in the lives of hundreds of Canadian engineers.

A few professors from the Faculty of Arts gave courses to the benighted Schoolmen. An incident involving one of these outsiders throws light on the conflicts that could develop. One of the members of our year had been severely shell-shocked and was totally deaf, but an expert lip-reader. He was very popular and could take part in normal conversation with anyone. We had attended several incomprehensible lectures in an arts subject one term when the professor suddenly turned from the blackboard and, pointing to our deaf member in the front row, asked a question. The professor wore a heavy moustache which completely concealed his lips. When there was no reply, he shouted another question, adding a stinging criticism of this person in particular and the class in general, ending up by ordering him from the lecture room. At this the whole class rose and left the room; nor did they return for more lectures by that professor. Later Professor Bain gave them three lectures on the subject. The students took the examination and, perhaps in remorse, the professor passed every one of them.

A certain amount of song was encouraged in those days at Hart House, but wine and women were definitely out. Women were, it is true, allowed in the university men's residences for Sunday afternoon tea, but all doors were left open and hours were limited. Despite such restrictions, however, the twenties were scarcely Victorian. They were years of prohibition and bootleggers, and many houses in the Huron Street area sold liquor to carefully identified customers. Amongst these were students of all faculties, and SPS had its share.

From this fact arose an incident in Hart House late one evening, when a group of merrymakers were apprehended by the night watchman. He requested them to leave immediately but they were by that time so emboldened as to refuse, and the party continued unabated. The incident was reported to the warden of Hart House, J.B. Bickersteth. Liquor was of course prohibited on all university property. The warden knew he must report the incident to Sir Robert Falconer.

Now, Mr Bickersteth, a front line soldier himself in the first world war and sympathetic to the veterans, realized he would have a problem in avoiding overzealous punishment by the very strait-laced president who was a prohibitionist by conduct and conviction. He recounted the story to Sir Robert, explaining that all the offenders had served overseas, that some had won rapid promotion as well as battle awards, and that now they were leaders on the campus. In spite of this the warden conceded that they should be punished for their misdemeanour, and proposed denying them all privileges in Hart House for three months.

Sir Robert disagreed emphatically: the warden was too lenient, he said, and the offence warranted suspension. In horror, the warden thoughtlessly interjected, 'But, Sir Robert, you know, everyone has been tight at least once in his lifetime.' Here the tide turned. 'Utter nonsense,' replied Sir Robert, and the warden became the accused. He was scolded for his casual outlook on drinking, especially at the university. But his recommendation nevertheless prevailed. This was only one incident whereby the kindly understanding of exuberant youth by Mr Bickerstith made him beloved by the student body. He served his students even as he served his university, and was totally dedicated to the office he held.

How did this mixed bag of veterans and non-veterans do in their examinations? At the time there was evidently some relief that things had gone better than might have been expected, for in his 1920 report the dean could say:

The academic feature of the past year has been the performance of the returned soldiers, who composed over fifty per cent of the attendance in the four years. Their work throughout the year and the results of their examinations indicated that they have been fully able to revive their studious habits after the strenuous years at the War, and in this they have surpassed even the best expectations in their diligence and serious application.

Their success was achieved, it might be added, in spite of overcrowded classes and insufficient equipment. Indeed, had it not been for these conditions, the rate of failure in the early twenties might not have been from 15 to 20 per cent. In any event, the rate dropped with new buildings, better equipment, and less crowding.

On the fortieth anniversary of their graduation, the Class of 2T3 expressed their feelings, perhaps mellowed over the years, by erecting a plaque (donated by George Beecroft) in the old Mining Building. It read: 'In grateful recognition of the outstanding ability and untiring devotion of the Staff of the Faculty of Applied Science and Engineering of the University of Toronto, 1919-23.' But when their degrees were fresh and new, the same class had many gripes, and bull-sessions were held on what should be done to improve the courses. The eventual result was a memorandum, submitted to the Faculty Council in September 1926 by the Toronto members of the class, following discussions over a two-year period. Eleven suggestions were noted in the memorandum, among them: that individuals should be offered guidance and advice by the teaching staff in choosing between courses; that matriculation subjects be eliminated from School courses, and a more thorough grounding be added in the higher mathematics; that a comprehensive course covering business management be set up replacing the then-independent series of lectures on non-engineering subjects; that professorships in the Faculty be created in all subjects then taught by members of other faculties; and that printed notes be distributed wherever possible at the commencement of lectures. Suggestions were also made with regard to the holding of periodic quizzes and the writing of seminar theses. Some years later Dean C.R. Young wrote the class to say that most of the recommendations had been carried out over time, and that where this had been impossible it was generally for practical reasons – usually lack of funds.

Not all the time and energies of the students were taken up with attending lectures and labs. The veterans in particular had their special concerns, and eventually formed a University of Toronto Veterans' Association, called Varsity Vets. The late Frank O'Leary, a one-legged Med, was president and C.T. (Terry) Carson, School '23, was secretary. A search for a worthy objective finally brought forth the idea of a war memorial honouring the university's graduates and undergraduates who had given their lives in the first world war. To start a fund a number of veterans got together and wrote and produced *The P.B.I.* ('The Poor Bloody Infantry'), a war play complete with the old songs, the old gags, the spy, and a rather good representation of the drama of a night raid with some heroism, and, alas, some deaths. The first performances were in Hart House Theatre. The show went on tour for two summers, played to enthusiastic audiences, and made some money – only a fraction of what was needed, but the Memorial Fund was launched. And so the veteran undergraduates of the twenties were responsible for the genesis of that most impressive memorial, the Soldiers' Tower, dedicated in June 1924, as well as the continuing benefits of a loan fund for needy students that was set up with part of the money collected.

The idea of a School stunt night which finally resulted in SPaSms sprang up during the 1919-20 year. 'Why should Meds have a stunt night and not School? Anything Meds can do, School can do better.' This chorus grew during the fall of 1920 until it won the sanction of the Engineering Society, whose president at the time was the redoubtable Ralph Downie. Men from all years took part in work on stage and behind the scenes. The character of the program is indicated by some of the acts: 'Laboratory Lapses' (by III Chemicals), 'High Bar Act' (Huestis and Co), 'Krazy Kabaret (III year), 'The Village Orchestra' (a skit by the Toike-Oikestra), 'The Eternal Triangle,' French Habitant Recitations (Ralph Kerr), 'The Adventures of Kloreen: A Gas Attack in One Wave' (IV Year Chemicals), Male Quartette (Walker, MacQueen, Maund, and Weldon), and, for the finale, the 'School Psalm.'

The many hours of rehearsing and performance that went into this show and others which followed suggest the satisfaction that the undergraduates of those days felt in getting away from the routine of classes and labs and finding a healthy outlet for their good spirits and good fellowship. The annual School Nights which followed were hilarious affairs of stunts and skits. On several such occasions a chariot race was held. The charioteers sat on chamber pots and were pulled around the race course, usually ending in a heap at the end. At the School Reunion in 1925, the Class of 2T3 decided to put on a full-dress presentation of a Roman chariot race. It was a sparkling success. First, Joe Dyer entered dressed as Caesar in the full regalia of an emperor, preceded and followed by dancing vestal virgins. Then the prancing horses appeared, pulling the two charioteers on chamber pots. The winner was presented with a crown of laurel leaves. Thus began the chariot race that took place yearly around the front campus.

Disturbances of one kind and another did of course occur but not, I suspect, as many or as serious as those of recent years. Most men who served in any theatre of war, in almost any capacity, imbibed a degree of respect for authority. The greater their responsibilities had been, the more sympathetic they were to the problems faced by administration: rank, so important in the armed forces, leaves its mark on the individual. Almost everyone in the first world war knew what it was to be told to 'wait for the word of command.' The large war year which graduated in 1923 was made up as follows: Army, 126; Navy, 4; Air Force, 35; Army and Air Force, 12; Navy and Air, 4; Miscellaneous, 27. Of these, 63 had been officers, including 8 cadets, and 22 non-coms. Some twenty had received decorations or had been mentioned in despatches.

The overtones of war experience were clear in an incident which took place in connection with a certain initiation. The latter was planned as a traditional affair, involving the imposition of many indignities upon the freshmen. The first-year president had been an infantry officer in the front line. When his class was requested to present themselves at the old gymnasium behind North House to be initiated, he rebelled. His military philosophy prevailed: why not attack rather than submit? He found ready followers amongst his classmates and organized them along military lines. The objective was to reverse the pattern – the freshmen would initiate the sophs.

His Intelligence Section ascertained the plan of the unsuspecting sophomores and reported that they would gather within the gymnasium where an assortment of properties for mild forms of 'welcome' would be set up. The waiting freshmen would be admitted at a controlled rate as fast as the treatment could be administered. 'Splendid.' no doubt said the hero of the plot; 'instead of the sophomores controlling our entrance, we will control their exit – but only as fast as we can initiate them.' Plans were made accordingly. One frosh division was to lock all the doors from the outside, except for one three-by-three-foot door at ground level which would be the control exit. Another division was to cut off all lights in the building, whilst a third injected just enough ammonia to make the sophomores willing to escape from the building as fast as they were allowed.

The evening arrived and the sophs gathered as planned. The freshmen did not arrive at the appointed hour. There was some apprehension at the delay. Still, no one took it seriously: freshmen had always submitted to hazing by their seniors. The first danger sign came when the light went out. This was followed by the shattering of an overhead skylight. A glass container of liquid ammonia crashed on the floor. In a short time the highly volatile, noxious solution permeated the building. When the choking inmates in complete darkness found the main doors locked, there was consternation. Those outside, hearing screams from within and the gasping of the few students allowed to crawl out, soon realized the seriousness of the situation and opened the large doors. A mass exit followed. Some of the victims dropped to the grass, but in a few minutes all had recovered. Then followed a rough unplanned initiation of the few freshmen who remained on the scene. Amongst them was their leader.

The tactic failed because the whole quantity of ammonia was dropped at one time, and it is doubtful that this was part of the plan. The student given most credit for this unprecedented event remained to get his degree and to become a distinguished citizen who contributed much to his community and once more gave outstanding service to his country in the second world war.

In contrast to this regrettable event was the soph-frosh confrontation of the preceding autumn, 1919. The freshman class, four hundred strong, made up in great part of men who had spent years in the war, were more amused than concerned when the much younger sophomores, with less than half their numbers, intimated a desire to hold an initiation. Eventually the freshmen agreed to submit, provided that those who had been casualties and were still in 'E' category could go through without physical contact. The sophs agreed. The freshmen met at the bandstand in the centre of Queen's Park and marched to the School building in alphabetical order. Dean Mitchell, who was honorory president of that year, insisted that he was a freshman and went through with the gang.

The election of fellow undergraduates to the many offices of the student body of SPS has long been a process that combines a bit of frivolity with the serious matter of choosing satisfactory candidates. The veterans of 2T3 had learned the lesson that community living must be organized and certain lines of authority established. It was logical that they should enter into the spirit of elections with all the enthusiasm that the occasion demanded and permitted. It is surprising how often we selected men who made their marks in later life..

The university community was as real to us as a municipality, and we had a responsibility to ensure that it was well administered. This does not mean that we did not extract a maximum portion of merriment in the process. Who can forget election night, organized ostensibly to announce the victors, but in reality a celebration in which a good time was had by all? Games were played those nights in the old drafting room behind Convocation Hall, and on one occasion in the course of the games one of the celebrators – an ex-soldier – lost his glass eye. Soon everyone was on hands and knees, like crawling ants, looking for the lost object. Before long it was found, wiped off with a handkerchief, and restored to its proper socket.

On another occasion, the election festivities being over, the crowd dispersed. As we walked across the front campus we heard the clanging of steel and a cry for help, 'Let me out, let me out!' Investigation revealed one of our number behind locked iron gates in front of the main entrance of University College. He claimed he had been incarcerated without reason. With our aid he was able to climb over the palings to freedom. We never knew how he got in there, and he wasn't telling!

Sports of all kinds took a high place in the regard of students in those days. The chant, 'We shout and fight for the Blue and White' poured forth in great volume, especially at rugby games. Individual encounters aroused wide interest. At one interfaculty assault-at-arms, the most spectacular event was a bout between champions of School and Meds, which it was expected would settle a long series of inderminate combats that had produced some feeling between the two faculties. The Schoolman knocked out the Med in the first round. After a period of astonished silence, his partisans exploded with a tremendous 'Toike Oike.'

Most of us were also proud of the achievements of Schoolmen in interfaculty, intercollegiate, and even wider competition. Schoolmen, for example, contributed to the outstanding Varsity senior rowing teams which won the Canadian eights championship in four consecutive years, from 1920 to 1923, and then went on to represent Canada at the Olympics in 1924. There the Blues beat Great Britain and Italy, and finished second only to the United States. Engineers were on all those teams. At the Olympics Art Bell, John Smith, and Boyd Little actually rowed, and Bill Thompson was a spare. We felt these efforts reflected glory and fame on School and Varsity.

Shortage of space prevents more details of awards earned and records established in many sports, or a recital of the 'T' and 'S' holders from School whose photographs may be seen in copies of *Torontonensis*. Participation by the players, supporters, and spectators was a constructive and unifying influence in those early days. Many players were able to combine sports with academic honours. But not all. Some paid the penalty for displaying too great devotion to their first love, much to the regret of other Schoolmen who were more mindful of the need to qualify for that elusive B A SC.

It is moving to study the copies of *Torontonensis* issued in the early twenties. The war was very much in the memory of those who wrote, and no doubt also the realization that many graduates and men who might have become students never came back. The opening salutation in the 1920 edition is from that thoughtful president, Sir Robert Falconer. His words, although addressed only to that year's graduating class, applied to all who received degrees throughout the first part of the twenties: 'Those who leave the university will face a world which is laboriously and painfully adjusting itself to the terrible confusion into which it was thrown by the practically universal war. One function of education is to produce the understanding mind, and wisdom follows on understanding.' The theme for the 1920 volume was 'Reconstruction'; that for 1921 was, more hopefully, 'Progress,' suggested by a flowing standard borne by a mounted knight. But Falconer noted in his address in that volume that 'we must interpret progress in terms of man's control of himself and the diffusion of those virtues which will make human society happier and more reasonable.'

Two questions were hopefully asked in a valedictory address in 1920: 'Will there be a broader and more tolerant outlook on national affairs?' and 'Is there to prevail a finer and more delicate social sympathy?' These questions no doubt reflected some concern in the minds of the more social-minded students. There was still hope for peaceful change, and not yet the feeling of later years that drastic measures were needed.

In a large university and a large faculty like School there are bound to be special groupings which form for different reasons. There are those in university residences, those in fraternities, those from the city who continue their associations with high school comrades. Then there are a certain number of loners, especially those from the country, who do not feel the need to belong to groups, who live in boarding houses and have little interest in obtaining residence accommodation or in active participation in the many university organizations.

Hart House probably meant more to out-of-towners than to those whose homes were in the city. In its many functions it served as a sort of melting pot, even a home, for students from different faculties, getting them acquainted with one another and acting as a unifying catalyst to bring about an awareness that they were all one in a great University of Toronto.

But in trying to recall those early postwar years and our experiences since, it would seem that it was the presence of so many returned men – who had lived through periods of warfare, even if in different forms and in various locations – that was the most important factor in unifying the classes of the early twenties and in building up the sense of good fellowship which has continued these many years.

This began even before our first term as undergraduates. To help men who were short of honour matriculation standing in mathematics, the university made available two 'prep' classes, one in the winter of 1918-19 and the other in the summer of 1919. Miss M.A.G. (Mary) Waddell conducted the classes in a sympathetic and efficient manner. They were held on the ground floor of University College. The men in these relatively small groups came to know and respect each other, and when the time came for the first-year elections, each group entered candidates for the various positions. As a result, two men from each group found themselves confronted with the responsibilities ot office. An expanded executive was formed, bringing in a number of other men, and a series of class events was planned and carried out. These activities, together with the work in drafting rooms and in small groups in labs, and the competitions in gym and playing field, resulted in the development of a spirit of comradeship between returned and non-returned men which strengthened class and School spirit.

Comments like these have been made: 'It was a great privilege for those of us who were not veterans to be members of a war year; though very much in a minority we at no time felt left out of the various activities!' or, 'As a non-returned man I felt some awe and admiration at being amongst so many returned men. This did not cause any complexes however.' And one retired senior executive wrote: 'Over the ensuing years I have many times recalled my good fortune at being in university while many of the first war veterans were there. I believe these men created a student mix that was most valuable to the younger fellows as they made university experience much broader than straight book learning, as it too often is. Several of these guided me through the maze of Hart House activities and what goes on beyond the class rooms. This naturally caused me to participate in areas outside of athletics and in so-called political university experiences open to all students.'

The valedictory address in the 1921 *Torontonensis* reflected the feelings of most of the students in School: that the years at the university presented 'unique opportunities for fellowship in matters social, intellectual and spiritual,' and to the extent that they took advantage of these opportunities they were the better for it.

How did the individual student feel as he approached his final examinations, and, if successful, the following Convocation? There is little doubt that most of them felt some concern regarding jobs. The dean noted the effort made in this connection in his 1923 report:

A new feature has been the revival of effort to assist the graduating class of the Faculty in obtaining positions. For this purpose a special organization was arranged in the spring months to get graduates in touch with possible employers. The funds required, though a small amount, have been derived from the University, the Alumni and other sources. This has been a marked success.

C.C. Rous will be remembered by many students who were helped by him in that and succeeding years.

But jobs were scarce. Something of a depression had set in, and as a result many new graduates had to seek employment in the United States. This situation continued for several years. In 1927 the Dean reported with regret that a considerable proportion of the graduation class had to seek employment outside Canada, but that this state of affairs had not been so marked as in the previous two years and there were indications that the situation was improving. In 1928 he could say: 'The graduating class this year was promptly absorbed in work within our own country, and there are many instances where graduates who, a few years ago, had found employment in the United States, have now returned to lucrative positions in Canada.' It was even better in 1929 when the graduating class was absorbed in Canada 'in an astonishing manner,' many members being offered two or more jobs. Happy days were here again, for a time at least.

However, this article has been concerned particularly with the years immediately after the first world war. To conclude, therefore, let us turn to the Special Convocation of 1923. In his report for that year, the dean introduced the subject on a cheerful note:

The very large fourth year, 253 graduating, has been unprecedented not only in numbers but in type, quality and ability generally. The average age is over twenty-five years and about 60 per cent have seen war service. It is interesting to note that these are distributed 40 in Civil Engineering, 20 in Mining, 56 in Mechanical, 54 in Chemical, 63 in Electrical, 8 in Metallurgical, and 12 in Architecture. A departure was made this year in holding the Convocation for conferring degrees in this Faculty as soon after the examination as possible, the first of May. This change was very satisfactory, and appears fully warranted as there were nearly twice as many present to receive degrees as has been usual at the June Convocation.

Here is a description of that event, written shortly afterward:

The section of the Hall on the lower level of the elevated portion facing the platform was reserved for SPS and a few graduates from OAC. The entire floor and the first galleries were filled with friends of the Year. The conferring of degrees was performed by the Chancellor, Sir William Mulock, Dean Mitchell presenting the aspirants. At the conclusion of the ceremony a mighty 'Toike Oike' gave the 'Amen,' and the joyful newly graduated and their proud friends and relations adjourned to the Draughting Room, scene of many a festival, for refreshments.

'There never has been such a successful Convocation; it must be repeated for each graduating year of School,' said the officials. But never again will there be the same Convocation exactly as the one in 1923 when the year that had occupied the stage in the giving of the play, *The Soldier Year at Varsity,* in four acts made its bow to the gallery, received its official blessing, and turned its steps to the wider sphere of life in the wide, wide world.

R.S. SEGSWORTH

The thirties

This was the period that began in a depression and ended in a war, both of which have been described as 'history's biggest'; and yet in retrospect it was not all that bad. Certainly we had problems, real problems, but one knew what they were and each person dealt with his as best he could. It is sometimes surprising to look back and remember that there was also real gaiety and laughter in those days, and many fewer long faces than are to be encountered on the campus now.

Life was more formal, Men wore collars and ties. A suit, with pants and jacket matching, was standard attire, even if patched. We wore garters to hold up our socks and braces to perform the same services for our trousers. Staff-student relations also tended to be a bit stiff and formal, one situation that has clearly improved over the years.

In the thirties even full professors were grossly underpaid and over-worked. In fact, it was so bad that the Toronto newspapers were able to uncover instances where the janitors were actually being better paid than some of the teaching staff. At that time, professors were expected to give ten to fifteen effective lectures per week as well as taking care of all the administrative and other work that fell to their lot.

Student loans, bursaries, and other aid were almost unheard of and money was really tight. It was commonplace for students to skip a meal, not because they were overweight, but simply for lack of funds – and this despite the fact that a good lunch could be obtained in the Great Hall at Hart House for about 35 cents. How well one remembers the tables set up with great pitchers of milk and seemingly unlimited supplies of good raisin bread!

This was an age when, on the campus, men were men and girls were girls and you could tell the difference. The boys had not yet attempted to imitate the female penchant for wide variety in colour and styles of apparel and hair. And even then girls were taking, and succeeding in, Engineering. There were four women undergraduates in an enrolment of 769 in 1930, and twelve in an enrolment of 961 by 1940. It is unfortunate that, despite Women's Lib and the example set by so many Russian women in this field, the numbers entering School have increased only very slowly. (In 1970 the proportion of women was lower than in 1940 – twenty-seven out of 2,199.)

We saw less of the girls in those days owing, in part only, to the fact that there were fewer of them on the campus in both absolute and relative numbers. They were, however, in general, much more beautiful and exciting than the current crop. (Some young engineers now on campus do not share this view.)

There was no parking problem around the university. Almost none of the students and for that matter few of the staff had cars. People walked or took the streetcar (four tickets for a quarter).

We took our social events seriously even when participation might mean real financial sacrifice. And we did enjoy these events, although they would seem to be dry and formal by modern standards. No winter session was complete without the School At-Home, School Night, the School Dinner and, for those fortunate fourth-year men, the Grad Ball. Oddly enough, even by fourth year, relatively few had steady girl friends and there was always a scramble for 'sisters and cousins' for relatively unattached Schoolmen to take to these affairs.

Initiations also were not taken lightly and it was the ambition of every second-year man to give the lowly frosh at least as much as he himself had received the previous year. Invariably, however, these affairs ended up with the fun and fellowship of dinner in the Great Hall at Hart House. Yet this did not prevent 'tappings' that might occur at any time and it has been reported that on one occasion even the dean got dunked, by mistake, by some highly embarrassed sophomores.

We did sing the School songs, often and lustily, and we quickly learned not only 'Columbo' but quite a few that were suitable for polite company.

Right smack in the middle of this period is the Class of 3T5, which modestly claims to be unique and has rarely overlooked an opportunity to advertise the fact. At least it had the good sense to elect as permanent class chairman Bob Hewitt, a man with enough initiative, charm, and wisdom to develop a class organization that has continued to be active and effective ever since. Possibly the very real and obvious problems of the thirties contributed to the forging of a special bond of comradeship. Perhaps also, as a result of their experience, the class quickly came to realize that the profession of engineering was much more than just an accumulation of technical knowledge and the development of skill and judgment in the application of this knowledge. In 1944 it established the 3T5 Second Mile Award for students in fourth-year engineering who demonstrate an effective concern beyond and outside the purely technical and academic part of their experience at the university. Over the years, this 'projection from the experience of the thirties' has continued to emphasize that 'human values and relationships are the most important element in any engineering project.'

In addition to sponsoring the Second Mile Award, members of 3T5 have continued to be active in university affairs. Jack Powlesland, for example, is a past president of the Engineering Alumni Association. At their regular monthly get-togethers class members continue endless discussions related to engineering and engineering education under such titles as 'Industry's Most Wanted Man,' 'Design in Engineering Education,' or 'What is Going on at School.' They have also participated actively in first-year design projects and in various engineering seminars with student groups and the teaching staff in the course of the regular School routine.

The thirties will be remembered as the period of Dean Mitchell, who said that 'every engineer is by nature an economist.' This was also the time when, under the influence of sheer exuberance (drugs were unheard of and liquor was scarce and expensive), a largish group of students paraded *en masse* into a famous downtown movie house without the formality of paying. The subsequent bawling out by the dean was the real highlight of the experience. There were shouting and snowball-throwing contests with Meds, and even (it is whispered) serenades and something referred to as a 'panty raid' on such prim and proper off-limits establishments as Annesley Hall.

The dean was very proud of School. He never ceased to comment on the fact that enrolment continued to increase despite rising admission standards. He was also proud of the staff and cited their accomplishments at every opportunity. Having done this, however, he invariably found an opening into which he would slip an eloquent comment about the need for expanded facilities. The physical plant then was limited to the old Schoolhouse, the old Electrical Building, and the Mining Building, and some of this space was at times shared with other faculties. Succeeding generations are indebted to this man who, more than anyone else, in the twenties and thirties kept up the pressure to maintain School's excellence. It was a herculean task, for times were tough and the primary demand on available resources was simply to keep people fed, housed, and clothed. Very little could be spared to expand higher education.

The depression struck suddenly. The Schoolmen graduating in June 1929 got jobs almost at once, but six months later most of them were out of work. The scars were to remain for many years. Numerous salary surveys have shown that those graduating in the depression years continued for some time at lower-than-average salaries in relation to their responsibilities and years of service.

There must have been some generally recognized special quality about School, for despite the depression enrolment held up remarkably well. There were, however, some wild swings in the distribution of students among the various departments, with consequent strain on the facilities. In 1931 the total registration was 848, with 12 graduating in Civil, 16 in Mining, 30 in Mechanical, 7 in Architecture, 33 in Chemical, 35 in Electrical, and 7 in Metallurgy. In addition some thirty students were registered in graduate work. In 1933 the total undergraduate attendance had grown to 913 and postgraduate registration had increased to 52.

By 1935 support for research had practically dried up. Nevertheless, in that year Professor H.W. Price of Electrical was awarded the McCharles Prize in recognition of his research and development work in the control of electrical power transmission systems. 1935 was also the low point in numbers, with 766 registered undergraduates.

In support of the contention that 'the more times change, the more they are the same,' it is interesting to note that in his 1938 annual report the dean found himself moved to remark that, 'notwithstanding the general unrest which is abroad, and the apparent unconcern and inattention of present-day youth to serious things, the young men of this faculty appear to have successfully resisted the slackness which seems so generally to prevail.'

By 1939 the undergraduate enrolment had increased to 925. Courses offered had increased during the thirties in total from about 300 to over 450, without, unfortunately, an equivalent increase in staff. At the end of '39 the latter totalled 150, including 39 professors, 14 lecturers, 9 instructors, and 40 demonstrators.

The school days were long – at least from 9 am to 5 pm five days a week and from 9 am to 12 noon on Saturdays, with usually three lab reports to write each week. During one term, T.R. Loudon gave a course of lectures on flying and aircraft design two mornings a week at 8 am. Electives were rare, and the curriculum did not provide any opportunity to take courses in the humanities or social sciences in other parts of the university.

In their fourth year, for example, the Civils carried six labs and thirteen lecture courses, while the Miners had eleven labs and eleven lecture courses, all without options. The Electricals were unique. Anticipating the future, they did have some choice, but in their last year only. It was possible for them to select two courses among hydraulic turbines, heat engines, illumination design, photometry, radiotelegraphy, and acoustics.

These were the years when everyone took surveying, and the Civils took it seriously. Survey camp at Gull Lake was a significant part of the curriculum, sometimes better remembered, however, for good times. Stories persist of great survey exploits, with traverses completed with errors of less than $3/8$ of an inch, all duly attested to on birch bark by no less an authority than Professor Treadgold himself. There have been vague references to a girls' camp located somewhere on the same lake, but no clear conection between this and the course of study set up at the survey camp has ever been established. Some enthusiasts claim the survey camp was the 'best five weeks at School.' In this connection, the 3T5 gang will be remembered for the tremendous crest painted on the ceiling of the lodge by one of their members, Art Pirttinen.

There were no study weeks at mid-term, but certain field trips did provide a welcome break. Somehow, expeditions arranged to provide exposure to such practical engineering feats as the power plants at Niagara Falls and Queenston got to be known as 'that trip to Buffalo.' Toronto was still outclassed in sophistication (and bargains) by its neighbour south of the border, and no engineer could consider himself educated without experience at the Buffalo Burlesque. Yet this particular course was never accredited.

Many people, both students and staff, contributed to the spirit and flavour of the times. Reference has already been made to the dean and to some other notable characters. There were many more.

J. Roy Cockburn was in his prime. In addition to his courses in descriptive geometry (and his figure skating), he could be counted on to give a lucid and entertaining talk seemingly on almost any subject and at the drop of a hat.

'Bobby' Angus told one joke only, in one lecture only, and to the fourth year only, but the shock was too much for the class and they only got around to laughing at it when reminded of the event years later. The story was about a bee who was swallowed by a bull. The bee fell asleep and when he woke up the bull was gone. There was an alleged reference in it to hydraulics.

Mechanicals remember Bob Wiren with deep affection. He was truly concerned, pleasant, and well informed. Although a member of a famous Russian noble family, he tended to be rather quiet and modest. He had escaped from Russia during the revolution and when he could be persuaded to talk about it the stories were wondrous.

Professor A.R. Zimmer taught electricity to practically everyone. After the first few days he could and did call everyone in the class by name. He could still do it if you happened to meet him years later. His concern for the Schoolmen under his care was very real and obvious.

Even thirty years ago, topics like pollution control and the wasting of natural assets were not overlooked. Very often Professor E.A. Allcut, with his hard facts, solid logic, and clear presentation, would be found leading discussions in this area.

Professor J.A. (Cawst Brawss) Newcomb, a fellow countryman of Professor Allcut, was a kindly man with a good sense of humour who, among other things, tried to extend some knowledge of elementary physical metallurgy to those outside Metallurgy.

These and others like them were truly the salt of the earth. Some in addition could add a touch of pepper. Practically everyone was exposed to a course in inorganic chemistry given by Professor E.G.R. Ardaugh. Many learned that in addition to his professional knowledge he possessed a temper controlled at times by what appeared to be a rather short fuse.

Professor H.E.T. Haultain retired in 1938, and in retrospect this seems to have initiated the phasing out of an era. There was a special spirit and loyalty among the Miners in his department. He occupied an office in the Mill Building for many years after retirement, from which he continued to exercise his influence over the Iron Ring ceremony. He also continued active participation in his technical field, and the superpanners and infrasizers which he developed found their way into many ore-dressing laboratories throughout the world.

C.R. Young had just taken over as head of Civil in 1929-30, following the death of Professor Peter Gillespie. His influence in the teaching of engineering extended far beyond his own department and will be warmly remembered by all who graduated in this and subsequent decades.

It is interesting to note that after all these years such men are remembered, not for the academic details of their courses, but for what they were. Personality and example appear to have been more significant than specifics of course content.

It must be remembered that in those days only the really advanced classes in electricity were involved in the magic of the vacuum tube. Computers were not dreamed of. Television, superhighways, worldwide air travel, high-rise apartments, systems engineering, nuclear power, the electron microscope, much of the synthetics and plastics technology, and a host of other developments were still to come. What did we do? What was there to study?

Detailed knowledge is a very transient thing. What is known for certain may be utterly wrong or completely supplanted by new knowledge within a few years. Engineering skill and judgment is timeless. No doubt those who were teaching in the thirties, like those who are teaching now, would be the first to admit that their efforts fell far short of their goal. Nevertheless the basic tools, language, graphics, mathematics, and the laws of physics and chemistry, were faithfully delivered to us. We did get, by example and drill, guidance and experience in the fundamental engineering function of overcoming a problem or achieving an objective by assembling data, assessing the data, exercising judgment, and taking action with integrity and honest effort.

Times were tough, it was hard work, but it was also fun and very much worthwhile.

ALAN HEISEY

The Ajax years

Sure'n a little bit of Hades
Rose from out the earth one day
And it settled on the lakeshore
Not so very far away.
And when the Faculty saw it
Sure'n it looked so bleak and bare
They said 'Suppose we grab it.
We can send the Skulemen there.'
So they sprinkled it with sliderules
As the Skulemen came in view
With here and there a demi
To give out a precious clue.
Now the DVA supports us
While we learn a million facts
Sure'n it never will be heaven
It's just U of T – Ajax!

As it tinkles back through one's memories, Garth McDowell's ditty from
a postwar Skule Nite says it all about the Ajax years. To the ancient
Greeks, Ajax was the god of war. To the Canadians of the early 1940s, Ajax
was a war-spawned defence plant. War had turned peaceful farmers' fields
twenty-five miles east of Toronto into a labyrinth of shell-filling plants cob-
webbed across a square mile of countryside. The hazards of the activity
required dispersing comparatively small, temporary, wooden buildings

well apart and connecting them by literally miles of spark-free, hardwood-floored, enclosed corridors. As the products of the fields of Ajax 'bloomed' on the fields of Europe, the costly peace they helped achieve released a pent-up demand for, among other things, engineering education for thousands of Canadian servicemen.

The wartime annual reports of C.R. Young showed little awareness of how large a postwar flood might want to take engineering. Only after D-Day was there an apparent awareness of just how overtaxed existing facilities might suddenly become. To the harried Faculty, then, Ajax looked like and was an 'instant engineering school'; within six months of vj-Day, a delayed freshman class of 1,400, 75 per cent of them ex-servicemen, began their engineering education. Surprisingly enough, as Dean Young's reports recognized, the old shell-filling plant of 446 acres and 111 buildings provided better accommodation for teaching engineering than did the venerable buildings on the city campus.

Accommodation for teaching purposes included 23 lecture rooms, one auditorium used in part for lectures, 14 drafting rooms, 7 chemical laboratories, a physics laboratory, a mineralogical laboratory, a storage and issue room for surveying instruments, and a technical library.

In most instances the lecture rooms are arranged to seat 108 students, and, except in the case of the auditorium, no more than 135.

The dean's report for that first postwar year also commented on the problem of staff:

The teaching staff at Ajax, both full-time and part-time members, totals 102, of whom 20 were provided by the Departments of Geological Sciences, Mathematics, Physics and Political Economy in the Faculty of Arts. The ratio of one instructor per fourteen students is low for an undertaking in which much personal attention had to be given to students, particularly to those who had been long in the services.

It is gratifying to report that despite the difficulty of finding in a short time so great a number of new members of the staff, the teaching is, in general, of high quality. Nearly twenty members of the staff served at one time or another as housemasters in residence and in this dual capacity contributed materially to the understanding between academic staff and students.

The dean did recognize the 'great distances' between buildings as a disadvantage. The real measure of that space could be experienced only on a cold winter's morning when one had just grabbed for and missed the last of the so-called green dragons. These were the bench-rimmed semi-trailers which served as austere commuter buses between the residences at the north end of Ajax and the onetime ammunition 'lines' along which the various teaching buildings were strung down towards Lake Ontario. After the last bus had left, the hardy could either hoof it diagonally across fields to far-off Line One, or else walk the longer, but drier, route through the connecting corridors of the lines in between.

Part of the special feeling of Ajax was the sense of belonging, not to Canada's largest university, but to a small, separate campus more the size of a maritime college. The big individual class years broke down for most purposes to eleven separate course sections. Some of the big sections, like Civil and Mechanical, broke down further into manageable, human groups for drafting and other labs and for life in the residences. Thus Ajax life was more informal and friend-creating than any fraternity could ever be, and free of the Greeks' self-estimation.

Perhaps we missed the traditional atmosphere of timeless Gothic piles. We surely did miss some of the advantages of inter-faculty intercourse on what is now known as the St George campus. But for vets and non-vets alike, Ajax in its plainness, its masculinity, and its overall flavour was reminiscent of some northern mining town or logging camp; and in its north-like isolation and its wartime utility setting we could share a feeling of being newer, of being apart, of even being uniquely relevant to the particular times we were a part of.

For one barely too young to have served in the war yet old enough to have known the war atmosphere as a teenager, Ajax was an intriguing way-station between war and peace. There was a military camp's drabness in the siting of the thirty-five residences (built for war workers) east and west down both sides of a gravel road. In my first year I drew '744' as a residence and only by hunking down the road did I learn it was the farthest bunkhouse from everything else.

Mine was a residence like all the others. It was spartanly furnished with two army-width beds to each room, six rooms or so on either side of a dreary hall, and two such wings connected in a U at the street end by a common room equipped with a radio, maybe a pingpong table, and a couple of wartime silkscreen scenes of Canada. Inevitably a few men wasted away their DVA credits playing endless bridge in the common room. For most of us, however, the main place for happy times was in the utility rooms halfway down each wing. These rooms were equipped with a refrigerator and hotplate, and many a cup of cocoa was drunk while help was given in solving a knotty assignment. The common rooms came into their own only when occasional residence dances were given, and busloads of insurance company or Bell Telephone girls were brought in from Oshawa or Toronto for a Thursday evening bash. 'A girl was taking her life in her hands to go to a residence dance,' one Ajax man recalls.

Some of the married vets managed to get houses in the war-built town of Ajax. Others commuted from Oshawa or Whitby or Toronto. Otherwise social life and education led out from a succession of residences, all super-heated by the black, insulated, hissing steam lines which connected them to the central power house. One of my classmates recalls setting up a hammer sequence through every radiator in his residence by knowing how to adjust the settings. (Appropriately enough, he went to work for Honeywell.)

A veteran student recalls how he and a number of others made repre-sentations after their first year about the practice of employing demonstra-tors as housemasters. They pointed out that many of the students had commanded battalions of a thousand men, and should be competent to look after a small residence. Thereafter many of the housemasters were veterans.

Only one house was different: 721 – closest to the mess-hall – was where the few lady students and lecturers lived, and only occasionally were the bent-necked lights over its front doors switched to red to reflect some student's humour. Perhaps the most imaginative prank carried out at Ajax was filling a student's room through its window right to the ceiling with straw, creating a different view for the owner when he opened his door. A more common prank, viewed very coldly by the university, was the fire-hose water fight between two residences. And it seems to me that at least one automobile was laboriously set on a residence roof.

Since the classrooms were at least as well fitted out as most on the main campus, the second most vital building after the residences was the cafeteria. Many are the tales still recalled about the meals and the kitchen wenches, particularly one famed in many a Skule Nite as 'Bedroom Eyes.' She worked behind the counter with her dark eyes always half closed. There was also the Irish setter named Big Red, and a legendary piece of meat that was jammed on the notice board with a fork as unedible to the hound or anyone else – and labelled 'fried thigh of kitchen wench.' There was sneaking a second milk out of the cafeteria under your tray, and fried bacon and powdered eggs which were cooked the night before and couldn't be brought back to taste by reheating, and parsnips that constituted the sec-ond vegetable for two solid months in the recollection of one of my closest friends – who claims he hasn't eaten them since – and grape fights which turned into general mêlées, and 'Tits' and 'Rivets' and the table-thumping when the first-named walked in.

After we slept, ate, and studied there was some time for recreation and we had our own Ajax Hart House with endless committees paralleling the big house on the main campus – and a cafeterial committee, of course. The vets tried unsuccessfully to get beer into Hart House but they were just ahead of their time. There was an active Engineering Society, which sponsored an Annual Dinner, operated the Ajax counterpart of the supplies store – one of my classmates still recalls Marie Critelli, whose bright smile while working in the store cheered up the boys – and ran the Engineering Society dance with the lads and their girls coming to the mess hall by special train for the evening from Toronto.

We had a library with Dean Perry's wife as the librarian. One memorable day a rumour went around that part of our English mark would be based on the number of books we had checked out, and the place was cleaned out in a flash. Near the library was a bowling alley and a barber shop – they'd go broke today – and a dry cleaning establishment. 'Shortreed Stadium' was a grassy field with a running track around it where football was played without benefit of cheerleaders. There was a sort of hobby shop where a ceremonial concrete tombstone cured over a cold night. And our water tower was regularly painted up with what would now be known as graffiti.

My academic recollections of Ajax, as of the main campus, are of a succession of scrambling efforts to stay above water. Others less terrorized by the first principles of differential calculus will thus recall the elements of engineering education more clearly than I. That my room-mate Gordy Mollenhauer devoted the night before the statics final to trying to teach me the fundamentals I do remember, and in the exam I wrote, crossed out, and re-wrote again solutions to the main problem. I emerged in a daze: Gordy never forgave me for pulling a 'second' while he got a 'third.' In a similar case, a 5T0 man stayed up all night to help a buddy prepare for his Christmas calculus exam, which the buddy passed and the helper flunked.

Out of the distant past some classes are recalled – most clearly, perhaps, Professor Wright's big English classes of three to four hundred. While the professor's special interest in Ajax students has become legend, so have the memories of his somewhat mechanical introduction to the basics of report writing, not excluding weights of paper. Coming right after lunch on a Thursday afternoon it induced a heavy sleep in one 5T1-er who recalls waking up to find everyone gone but the professor, who was leaning over him suggesting that perhaps he was wasting his time taking that course.

Other names one recalls include 'Gunboat' Hughes, who enlivened dynamics with plots involving ships, torpedoes, tracks, and other war-related elements. And Carson Morrison, who described the details of a Montreal bridge failure on which he had been asked to consult, and got assorted calculations on assorted beams checked by his classes.

I remember a little, doughty Belgian drafting instructor who used to urge us to be 'seemetrickal.' And the nasty practical joke of reversing the title-block rubber stamp in relation to the flat side of the stamp handle. More than one struggling draftsman, trying for a seven when he had been averaging a five, imprinted the stamp upside down in the corner of his completed drawing, to ensuing gnashings of teeth.

Marcus Long's philosophy classes were a real taste of the liberal arts, still exceptional in now-hazing memories. It is surprising how thinly my Ajax chums recall course titles, let alone the profs and the contents, after more than twenty years. One of them summed up most of the Ajax faculty, perhaps not unreasonably, as consisting of the 're-treads' (the older teachers who had delayed retirement to help out), the returned vets, and the demis, some of whom were younger than many in their classes. Perhaps the single most jarring intellectual experience at Ajax occurred after J. Roy Cockburn stopped teaching descriptive geometry. He used to give only two final examinations, which were alternated from year to year on the principle that a student who could pass either one understood all the principles. The first year after his term the pattern continued. The second year it was changed without notice, to more of the gnashing noted previously.

The veterans in our classes were in my memory the most distinctive element about Ajax. They were a little older, a little more serious, I'd even say a little wiser than the rest of us, for they had been everywhere, and had done many things we would only read about. It took a lot of prying to get wartime experiences out of them, since they seemed generally anxious to forget and get on with making new lives for themselves.

I do remember tall, quiet, moustachioed George Robertson telling me how a crewmate had saved his life and had given his own in the process. George was bailing out of a burning bomber over Germany when his flightboot caught in a flare chute by the hatch. He hung in space till the crewmate took the time to kick the boot free. George's chute opened in time and the other fellow's didn't. There were many more such stories if only one could get the vets talking.

Talk they did, however, about hair-raising episodes in Brussels brothels and of gals eating chocolates when they should have been participating. There was one curly-haired Air Force vet who was having a tough time adjusting to the Ajax academic life, whose eyes used to glaze as he'd recall that girl in India who made his nights so entertaining ... at least it sounded entertaining, the way he told it! He left at Christmas to go back to look for her.

Then there was economical Harold Cook with his own formula for low-cost textbooks. He simply bought them used at the beginning of the year and sold them again at the end. I've often wondered if education costs wouldn't have been lower in the intervening years with more of this approach.

While a lot of the vets wore pieces of old uniforms, all with one exception had been cleared of symbols of rank or bravery. One guy kept his DFC on his battle jacket and became known as 'D.F. Foo' for his vanity. The vets were great guys as far as I was concerned, like older brothers to a student who didn't have one. With a few noteworthy exceptions they found the transition from war to peace surprisingly easy. Morley Callaghan was commissioned to write a piece on their experience and came out to Ajax to interview some of them. He was disappointed to find that they didn't wake up screaming with memories of times past, and really had very few neuroses to build a feature around. He probably didn't hear what was an unwritten policy at Ajax: no first-year veteran student ever failed his year, and he was given some benefit of the doubt in his second. In his third year he was on his own.

The vets tended to cluster together to a certain extent. The Ajax chaplain, Carl Swan, was an ex-service Padre who attracted great friendship and affection from many of them and from non-vets as well. For some, the military setting of the old powder plant protracted the service atmosphere to eight or more years away from normal civilian life. For men such a long time away from the disciplines of the scholar, life in a bunkhouse with others suffering the same transition was much easier than if they had been living in lonely boarding houses on Huron Street. There was a sub-group among the vets which met occasionally at the local watering hole, the Spruce Villa, near Whitby. They became known as the Ajax Bombing, Gunnery and Rocket-Launching Society in a satire of the old RCAF training schools. I lacked the thirst and the gongs necessary for membership in such an august group, but the stories of evening 'missions' when they got together and 'launched rockets' were legion.

Those of us who came to Ajax directly from high school organized our own trial by fire of a sort, called 'the stag.' These were fabled evenings at the Rouge Hills Golf Club which had to be experienced to be believed. The various courses competed to see which could throw the best party with the best strippers and the dirtiest movies. My section, Engineering and Business, had some difficulties arranging for suitable talent and films since

Johnny Bahen of Civils had a lock on the best movies. However, stags were considered essential as deculturalizing events, and so we found other sources. We were a little casual about permits and ended up buying beer under age, selling it to minors, renting raunchy flicks, and staging a sadly ungraceful, hefty dame as our stripper for the evening. One of my contemporaries has reminded me of the balcony which ran around the hall upstairs and the trouble we had keeping the lads away from the artist's changing room. But I had happily forgotten all that.

What I have never forgotten was how obstreperous the classmates and others got when the stripper (or was it the film?) was considerably delayed. They began punching assorted holes in the walls of the club house, which were made of that crumby fibreboard and no test at all of their muscles. Even the big football players we had asked to be bouncers got into the act until we reminded them of their obligations, and the bartenders who roomed across the hall also got well into their work.

The surest proof that the above is factual is that Dean W.J.T. Wright, who kept all 2,500 of us under control most of the time, had your scribe in his office the following morning to answer to damage details supplied by the now-not-so-friendly innkeeper. Our club paid out some $75 to repair the walls, and to ensure that its executive would have no more direct contact with law and order.

Aside from the sheer size of our classes, the concentration of outstanding officers and other ranks from the war years gave a quality to Engineering Society meetings and social functions that any normal year would have a hard time equalling. This showed in a typically small way after we made the move to the much more impersonal main campus for our third and fourth years. One of the many talented arrivals, Paul LaPrairie of the redoubtable Class of 1950 – 'the men of the half-century,' they called themselves – appointed himself 'Director of Cultural Activities' to the Engineering Society. Paul used his Irish Regiment of Canada contacts to appropriate some surplus band uniforms and form the now historic Lady Godiva Memorial Marching Band. Probably the band's first major engagement was to play 'Where, oh, where has my little dog gone?' at the chariot race. It soon became a fixture at all major campus music and cultural events, such as the Skule 'Whorrer' House, set up in honour of some obscure event in a tent on the front campus.

'Doc' Stonehill and Ron Drinkwater of 5T1 Aeronautical Engineering moved surely into control of the typewriters producing the *Toike Oike*. Their most famous headline read, 'Skule wins in tomorrow's chariot race.' Stonehill, one hopes, has lived up to the future he cast for himself in *Toron-*

tonensis: 'I intend to maintain my standing as a gentleman and a scholar and a fine judge of the cheaper brands of rye, as there are damned few of us left.'

Probably LaPrairie's greatest escapade was to steal the famous dragon-shaped newel post from the foot of University College's eastern stairway as a reprisal after UC had stolen our cannon. I can still recall him snickering at the rear of his ramshackle band as they rabbled north across the campus chanting, 'We want our cannon. Give us our cannon.' One UC official was reported to have become so exercised over the theft that he phoned the president about it. Sidney Smith suggested that simply giving back the cannon might produce the dragon, and of course it did. But before the trophy actually was returned, by way of *The Varsity* office and in a box labelled 'From the P & O T Girls,' a false alarm was raised with a box of sawdust.

Ken Tupper was the tall, spare dean of Engineering in those days. I remember him for a true engineer's gambit. As an engineering student years before, he had decided to memorize the value of pi to ten decimal places. He then had the good luck to have a prof ask him in class to give the value of that constant: what one-upmanship the response must have been! Tupper always struck me as a man who found the slow-grinding mills of endless faculty committees excruciatingly slow. His comparatively short stay on campus suggests that this was indeed the case. But while he was there his living room was the setting for an Engineering Society executive tea one Sunday afternoon at which my own most satisfying student prank had its origins.

The Canadian and World Peace Congresses then were in full cry trying to ban the atomic bomb, and I had let my name get on their mailing lists. One bulletin to 'members and friends' announcing an election meeting arrived just before the dean's tea. I suggested that we all join up and vote. About fifty Engineers showed up in a ratty little basement room of UC one lunch hour shortly afterward to confront some six or eight *bona fide* members with requests for membership. We called the Toronto dailies too, and they showed up. The upshot was a story in *Time* magazine about the world's first non-communist peace-front organization. We voted all the membership fees to the Red Cross, and one of the boys who knew someone in the Mounties ensured that they got the facts straight on who were party sympathizers – and who just liked a good party.

As these paragraphs suggest, the transition to the main campus was an easy one. For those of us who were Torontonians, it meant giving up the by-now-romanticized pleasures of Ajax residence life for hitch-hiking to the campus from wherever we lived around the city. It also meant going to the freshman dance at the Drill Hall on St George Street as third-year men and old pros. I still remember this dance with some satisfaction, for I met a sweet little blonde from Whitney Hall in her first week at college and she's now the mother of my three kids. There's no question that the girling was profoundly better on the main campus than it ever had been for those determined few at Ajax who used to chase the cafeteria wenches.

It may seem ungenerous to recall, but many of us were disappointed in the calibre of much of the instruction we had in the final years. At least we put our time where our tempers were, however, and over the summer following graduation in 1951 the regulars of 'Sigma Phi Alpha,' a small group within our Engbiz year, sat down and did one of the most thorough course reconstructions any students have ever undertaken. It is noteworthy that six of the sixty of us in the class liked the business side of our studies enough to do postgraduate work in business administration in the United States. The Korean crisis was on at the time, and although it may seem hard to conceive now, some ten of the same small class went to work for old mother Generous Electric. This gross over-hiring led to the inevitable consequence within the next few years, but the story of our individual and collective career wringouts is one for another day.

It was the exceptional fellow at graduation who didn't have three or four job offers to choose between, rather a far cry from the thirties, or the seventies for that matter. Employers would pay our expenses to Hamilton for the day, give us IQ tests, let us be interviewed by dozens of their top brass, offer some of us jobs, and then take all of us to a big dinner at night. A fellow has to try baked Alaska for the first time somewhere, and Procter and Gamble was as good a place as any. Yet I've often wondered what P and G thought about our IQ scores that day. It was the only time I've ever been in a room with twenty other men all taking the same silly test and unsupervised. We naturally felt we should develop collective answers. Perhaps we were the smartest *group* ever!

The mood of the days of Ajax was a very different one from that prevailing today. It was the inevitable winding down of the wastes and passions of a cruel war, which some men now amazingly suggest had been the beginning of the 'industrial strength' of the country. This seems to me the same pernicious kind of semi-justification as 'scientific fallout' which is still used to justify the massive wastes of military and space expenditures.

Perhaps the following paragraphs by Sidney Smith, from the April 1949 issue of the *Varsity Graduate,* recapture as well as any the Ajax reality in a flourishing prose that is no longer in style.

'Ajax Division.' It is a proud name taken from the flagship of Admiral Harwood in his victory over the German battleship, *Admiral Graf Spee*. The Division was boldly designed during the summer of 1945, in a mood of indebtedness to our Armed Forces, to serve thousands of men and women who defended so gallantly our country and the ideals that we hold most dear. In fulfilling its high purpose, the Division afforded to nigh five thousand ex-service personnel an opportunity to prepare themselves for comparable service to Canada in the arts of peace. The Division has been worthy of its name.

The Crest, taken from a forward turret of HMS Ajax and presented in 1948 by the Admiralty to the University, is a badge of the qualities that are of the very stuff of our British heritage: initiative and resourcefulness, courage and valour. The Crest ever will be in the University frontispiece of one of the most brilliant chapters in the story of its progress. That chapter in part has been written by a gifted and devoted staff and by a student body of unexcelled calibre – men and women tested in the cruel lessons of war and trained and qualified in the Ajax Division for the exacting tasks of peace. Notwithstanding the closing of the Division, the Ajax chapter will not be completed as long as the Unversity endures!

Ajax (*we* never called it the Division) *is* a dream. I know for sure because circumstances took me back there a couple of months ago to speak to a class at the Ajax High School. The school stands on a modern street in a modern town right where we used to go to school and sleep and eat. The students evinced a polite passing interest when I mentioned the Engineering school, and the Bombing, Gunnery and Rocket Launching Society, and the old Ajax song. I secretly hoped they'd want me to sing them a chorus for old times' sake, but their concerns were with today and tomorrow. Which is as it should be. I guess.

ERIC J. MIGLIN

The recent years

The latter years of the sixties saw a virtual transformation of the Faculty of Applied Science and Engineering. On the whole, the fifties and early sixties had been happy years for the student, who upon graduation could select the job of his choice from the whole industrial range. Technologically, these were boom years and they created a demand for great numbers of engineers, which the university had no difficulty in meeting. After 1968, however, the job market became much less buoyant. Although his problem was not nearly so acute as that faced by his counterpart with an Arts degree, the graduate of Engineering – for the first time in many years – had seriously and conscientiously to hunt for work. By the seventies the sellers' market was over; no longer was the engineering degree an automatic passport to a good professional job.

While most Engineering graduates did find jobs, many discovered that they had to lower their sights substantially when the time came to decide which one to accept. Justifiably or not, the graduate felt himself over-trained and over-qualified for many of the positions he was being offered and he found that employers were not always prepared to use the high-powered techniques that he had been taught – altogether, a frustrating and disheartening situation. Concern over finding a job after graduation and the difficulty of matching that job to his expectations were the two problems that weighed most heavily on the mind of students as the Faculty approached the end of its first one hundred years of activity.

At the same time, the attitudes of the Engineering student towards employment were themselves altering. The type of work in which he was interested was broadening, in part because of the shortage of the more traditionally defined positions. More significant perhaps, an increasing number of students saw themselves seeking something other than a hard-core engineering job; and after four years of professional training, many found that they were able to enter a wide diversity of fields within the business community. A number of Chemical Engineering graduates, for example, turned to selling computers for IBM. The student was beginning to see his undergraduate training as simply a stepping-stone – a basis for the practice of engineering but also for work in such areas as business administration, law, and even medicine.

The Canadian engineering student at this time was part of the 'new generation.' Most had been born after 1950, had been raised in relative affluence, and had not lived through a war or a depression. In contrast to the two preceding generations and for obvious reasons, they had no desire to rebuild what had been destroyed and, not having experienced poverty, the pecuniary rewards of employment also meant less to them than to their predecessors. They were planning careers with their individual interests in mind, motivated by personal enthusiasm or devotion to a social concern. The engineering graduate of the early seventies was seeking a way to satisfy his own needs as well as fulfilling the needs of society.

The importance of ecological preservation and of curbing pollution had caught the public eye; engineering and technology were coming under fire as the root causes of many of the problems of the environment. The engineers and technologists who had been heralded as the builders of our society were now being denounced by some as wreakers of ecological havoc. No engineering student could help but be influenced by such invective; he began seriously to question the role of the engineer within society. He became interested and involved in the problems of the environment and he learned to be aware of the ecological implications of the work he might be doing. A number of engineering students worked for such organizations as Pollution Probe at the University of Toronto, on both a full-time and a volunteer basis during the summer. Some did research into such areas as urban waste and industrial pollution; others worked to publicize the seriousness of the pollution problem.

One group of engineering students attacked the problem of automotive pollution. With the help of the departments of Mechanical and Electrical Engineering, they designed and built an innovative and highly successful anti-pollution vehicle. 'Miss Purity,' an electric hybrid car built from the ground up, could be run on either propane gas or electric power. She became the Unversity of Toronto's entry, and one of two from Canada, in the Transcontinental Clean Air Car Race from Boston to Pasadena in the summer of 1970. She finished the race in a tie for first place in the hybrid electric class and runner-up for the top award. These successes led to the organization of a new project team to design and build an electric urban vehicle for the Urban Vehicle Design Competition in the summer of 1972.

Despite these contributions, public criticism from a number of quarters continued to suggest that engineers lacked a sense of social resposibility. The blame was laid on the manner in which they were educated; the Faculty was said to be producing a non-thinking technician who lacked any sense of social conscience. While the reaction to these attacks within the Faculty was that they were unjustified, the criticism forced both students and professors to take a hard look at themselves and at the kind of education being offered. An engineering education, it was generally agreed, should and could do more than train people to fit into the slots of the technically oriented jobs required by industry to fill its 'needs.'

Looking back on the sixties, there is no doubt that, both inside and outside the confines of the Faculty, traditional ideas and attitudes were changing. The curriculum was increasingly broadened and liberalized. Industrial Engineering and a number of the other departments began to emphasize the importance of the so-called 'soft engineering' topics such as human factors engineering. The course of studies became less rigid as the number and diversity of elective subjects was increased. The student was also being given much greater opportunities to register in courses offered by departments other than his own and even by other faculties in the university. The new flexibility made it possible for the student, especially in third and fourth year, to design a program which suited his personal interests and future plans.

In 1971-2, a major change occurred with the institution of a term system based entirely on half-year courses – again adding flexibility to the system. Initial student reaction to this change was unfavourable because final examinations now had to be written in both December and April – the new system ensured that the student would work continuously during the entire academic year, instead of beginning the big push in mid-February. But disappointment over the extra examination load was more than compensated by the freedom to share an Arts class or two with students of the opposite sex.

Also at this time the first experimental inroads were made in project-centred learning. Limited numbers of students were given the opportunity to design and build projects of their own. The Cockburn Unit in Engineering Design, funded by the J. Roy Cockburn Bequest, became a forerunner of this type of multidisciplined educational experiment.

The Galbraith Building, new headquarters of the Faculty
of Applied Science and Engineering, was opened in the
spring of 1961.

The new Engineering Stores.
Opposite: R.R. McLaughlin, dean from 1954 to 1965,
with a bust of the first dean in the foyer of the Galbraith
Building.

In 1966, the Schoolhouse fell before the wrecker's hammer. Four years later, a memorial plaque was unveiled on its former site, now occupied by the Medical Sciences Building, by the president of the Engineering Alumni Association, F. Ted Gerson, and Dean James M. Ham.

In the late fifties, initiations became constructive. Instead
of hazing, freshman work parties were organized – in
this case to clean up the Toronto Island beaches. But
some things remain constant, among them the roar of the
Cannon and the security measures surrounding it.

The Lady Godiva Memorial Band puts the official stamp on a Homecoming lunch in the Great Hall of Hart House.

The vehicles may change, and the weather,
but the Chariot Race goes on.

School spirit has picked up some fancy trappings over the years, but the real spirit of the Faculty has always been in its labs and classrooms. The laser burst above opens a five-page sampling of the look of Engineering at Toronto today.

The Faculty has long been concerned with conserving
the environment, whether through control of atmospheric
pollution, or efficient use of waterways, or the innovative

'clean-air' hybrid motor car 'Miss Purity,' designed and
built by staff and students for a prize-winning journey
across the continent.

Applied Science today has many faces, whether it is the study of molecular properties or of human engineering or (*above*) the team at the Institute of Aerospace Studies which made key calculations that helped bring the Apollo 13 astronauts back to earth (Ben Etkin, who became dean on 1 July 1973, is at the photo's far right), or the AECL miniature nuclear reactor baptized Slowpoke.

The little red Schoolhouse rose once more, in cardboard
effigy, at the undergraduate ball which heralded the
Faculty's centennial in March 1973.

These progressive steps were in the whole enthusiastically received by the student body. There was a general consensus that being allowed to participate in the academic programs of other departments and faculties broadened one's education and therefore was a step towards producing a better engineer. The teaching staff were also enthusiastic about the new educational approaches. There was a sense of unity, both in purpose and direction, within the Faculty with regard to the changes that were taking place – a sense of unity that could not always be found in other sectors of the university.

Just as technology and the engineering curriculum became modified under the pressure of social demand, so too did the role of the university student. The student who was caught up in a concern for the problems of society, and who planned a career of social usefulness, no longer adopted the free-wheeling, 'collegiate' style which characterized the fifties and early sixties.

The difference was most readily apparent in the campus social scene. Many of the traditions and activities that formed fond memories for old graduates disappeared. Gone were the gala events that had once been held at Hart House. Gone were many of the big social events that colleges and faculties had once sponsored. Gone were the Winter Carnival and the Homecoming celebrations. Gone was the intense interest and enthusiasm that intercollegiate athletics had once been able to generate. Gone for all intents and purposes was the Blue and White Society; 1971 even saw the dissolution of the Blue and White Band. Initiations, which had in earlier years helped to create an *esprit de corps,* a sense of belonging, gradually lost favour. They became 'constructive' – raising funds for cystic fibrosis or doing work at Hart House Farm – and took on the name 'Orientation.' The entering freshman was no longer harassed and made fun of; he was introduced instead to activities that were designed to help him adjust to campus life. This attitude was generally recognized as a change for the better.

The undergraduate community was no longer the closely knit body it once had been. The student did not identify with his 'home' college or faculty as he previously had done. Even the Engineers, while still one of the most cohesive bodies on campus, did not have the sense of togetherness, of 'oneness,' that formerly existed. This apparent lack of spirit and unity could clearly be seen in the virtual disappearance of the friendly interfaculty rivalries that once were at the centre of campus vitality. Medsmen and Engineers no longer engaged in raids or free-for-all snowball fights; no one attempted to kidnap the Skule Cannon. There was also a decreasing interest in interfaculty athletics. Except for those actually participating, most students felt no pride in belonging to the faculty which fielded the best football or hockey team.

The fading emphasis on the importance of maintaining social and athletic traditions was indicative of a basic change in ideas and attitudes. The university student was in many ways less spontaneous and carefree than his predecessors. He tended to take himself more seriously; he was more self-conscious and more concerned with his own level of maturity, he was less able to have fun by letting loose and doing something a trifle foolish, less able to laugh at himself. He tended not to depend on student antics to relieve daily pressures. Each successive freshman class possessed a greater self-image of maturity and sophistication. This air of self-confidence, coupled with the restless desire to help rid society of ills created by technology, created a new campus atmosphere.

Ironically, the growing complexity of the University of Toronto itself was partially responsible for the dilution of the sense of community. It had become a multiversity. The campus was no longer the centre of life for the student. He was acquiring his education at the university, but he looked elsewhere for his extracurricular activities. He had greater mobility and greater affluence than students before him. He expected to be entertained by the offerings of the big city; it was easy to see why there was an exodus from the campus once classes were over for the day.

Many of the events that had once been highlights of the Faculty's social calendar were no longer scheduled. Skule Nite had fallen along the way, as had similar theatrical productions in other colleges and faculties; there was no longer the interest or enthusiasm to sustain such shows. The Skule Dance, for years a major social event, was finally done away with in 1970 because response was so poor. For a number of years the informal 'hustling dances' held after the Blues' football and hockey games had been highly successful, but they too were discontinued. By 1971 only the Grad Ball and the Cannonball remained of the major social events, and even the latter was no longer the affair it once had been. The antics of the Brute Force Committee were still amusing, but the capers and raids they organized drew less and less enthusiasm each year. Gone were the days when the LGMB and BFC could at a moment's notice mobilize huge masses of Engineers for a fun-loving demonstration.

Campus social events which were dry in an alcoholic sense could not compete with the big-city lifestyle of the students. The lowering of the drinking age to eighteen in the summer of 1971 made it much easier to obtain liquor licences on campus and may have begun a revival of on-campus social activities. In the year following the change in the liquor laws, any event with a licence and the promise of reasonably priced beer was an instant success.

The football weekend suffered, although to a lesser extent than the social scene. There was a time when a Blues' game at another university would draw a large crowd of supporters for a riproaring couple of days out of town. The McGill game had been a special favourite. Monday morning after a McGill weekend would find the Engineering Stores overflowing with loot – street signs, flags, and other souvenirs 'liberated,' often in broad daylight, from the city of Montreal. The weekends were still as wild and wanton in the seventies, but the exodus was considerably smaller.

The first autumn of the seventies saw the last McGill weekend. As usual, there was less interest in the football game itself than in roaming and ravaging the host city. That year all parades were banned in Montreal in the wake of the FLQ crisis – yet the LGMB and its supporters marched down the main street around noon on a busy Saturday. The police obviously were not worried about the group's political leanings, but one diligent motorcycle patrolman tried nevertheless to issue the band a ticket for staging an illegal parade. He was stymied when no one would acknowledge being the leader of the procession.

The following year, the McGill football team was disbanded, but the ever-resourceful Engineers staged a 'McGill weekend' anyway. This time it was in Canada's capital city for a game against the University of Ottawa. What a weekend that was! Late Friday night, a crew of Skulemen staged a commando raid on the Ottawa locker room and painted all the team's equipment blue and white. The whole capital was given the once-over, with even the Parliament Buildings liberated of a few choice signs. Prime Minister Trudeau himself was fortunate; he never knew how close he came early one morning to losing the sign marking his place of residence at 24 Sussex Avenue. The following week the Engineering Society executive trembled at the prospect of a visit from the RCMP in search of missing memorabilia.

Through the years, the Lady Godiva Memorial Band has increasingly become a Faculty focal point, representing and symbolizing Engineers. But the rest of the university has also appreciated their existence. Some facets of campus activity continue to draw students from all faculties together – few can resist the LGMB.

The Band has always been made up of a hard core of dedicated Skulemen, some of them quite talented musicians who spent so much time on musical jaunts and escapades that one wonders how they ever kept up their studies. In recent years, the LGMB was constantly being invited to play at various events – including alumni dinners, campus dances, and Santa Claus and Grey Cup parades. Even when it was not invited to a function, it often went anyway. It thus performed at several 'official opening' festivities throughout the city in the firm conviction that no opening was truly official unless the LGMB assisted.

One such gala occurred in the summer of 1971 when Ontario Place first opened its gates to the public. The LGMB, although uninvited, was in attendance. Naturally, it did not stoop to pay admission, believing that it should get as much as it gave – free entry in return for a free concert; but this point totally escaped the surprised but stubborn provincial police officer at the gate. Undaunted by such a minor hindrance, the Band prowled the lakeshore. The site was still under construction: they managed to borrow transportation from some workers. Fortune had smiled once more upon the musicians, their instruments, and their girlfriends. The Lady Godiva Memorial Band arrived in triumph to supervise the opening of Ontario Place on a garbage scow.

One event that always drew a packed house in these years was the annual Engineering Slave Auction where some of the best-looking girls on campus were auctioned off for charity. Even though increasing abuse was heaped on the auction by *The Varsity* and the university's Women's Caucus, it continued to be a perennial success. With the new morality, it also became more and more *risqué* each year. For the auction of October 1971 the Mechanical Engineers of 7T3 secretly hired a stripper from the Victory. There on the lecture table in Old Physics 135 she did her thing – right down to the buff in front of three hundred unsuspecting Engineers. The place went wild.

While the Women's Caucus loudly complained of abuses, other women were more quietly and usefully modifying Engineering life. The Faculty was no longer a male bastion. The number of women students steadily increased. Although there were only forty in 1971, their presence helped to brighten up classes and served to remind the supposedly dehumanized technologists that education need not be merely endured. Some might have thought it an enviable position for these women to be surrounded by men, but the odds of sixty-to-one were sometimes a trifle overwhelming. A fair number of them could be found retreating to the Women's Common Room on the second floor of the Galbraith Building to pass their lunchtimes in all-female company. Total integration would take some time. Nevertheless, most women became quite active in the Engineering Society and in other student organizations. They also organized their own activities, even to the extent of fielding girls' hockey and basketball teams.

Although the Engineering students recognized the internal changes developing around them, the rest of the campus had its view of the Faculty funnelled through an unlikely source – *Toike Oike*. The *Toike* at this time was publishing on an almost regular bi-weekly basis, thereby creating a running rivalry with *The Varsity*; with 18,000 copies per issue, only a thousand fewer than its rival, *Toike Oike* was generally acknowledged to be the most widely read newspaper on campus. One could never find extra *Toikes* lying around the day after distribution, as one often found *The Varsity*. The *Toike* circulation extended beyond the University of Toronto campus to York University, Ryerson Polytechnical Institute, and the high schools. Rumour had it that there was even an avid reader in the upper echelons of Queen's Park: Premier Davis is known to have sent the staff a Christmas card.

While the editorial page sometimes contained scathing attacks on *The Varsity* and the Students' Administrative Council, *Toike Oike* was basically a humorous newspaper. The university had developed a stereotyped image of the Engineer away from his classes – for him, life was supposedly nothing but wine, women, and more women. The *Toike,* with the intention of entertaining the reader, helped to perpetuate this image through suggestive pictures, off-colour jokes, and outrageous cartoons. Although the stereotype was ill-suited to the majority of Engineers, less humorous practitioners of campus journalism took *Toike Oike'*s excesses seriously. The outlandish image was thrust on all Engineers indiscriminately; luckily, they responded with characteristic generosity and forgiveness.

Through all of this frolicking, the Engineering Society, as the official organization for the undergraduates in the Faculty, was beginning seriously to consider facets of university life other than the purely social. Faced with the changing interests of its members, it began to redirect and broaden its activities. In 1971-2, a new constitution was drafted which represented a major reorganization.

One of the areas which demanded much of the Society's attention was that of education. Engineering students were becoming seriously concerned about the type and quality of the education they were receiving. Course unions were organized in most departments; students made critiques on both the content of their courses and the teaching methods of their professors. Even though the results were often critical, most departments supported such student evaluation as a means of improving courses and bettering the quality of teaching.

Students at this time were becoming more and more involved in the academic and administrative decision-making of the Faculty. They were consulted to a greater degree than ever before by their professors, by their departments, and by the Faculty officers. Their advice and comments were sought both informally and formally. Virtually every department had a number of committees, such as an academic planning committee, on which students actively participated. By 1970 the Faculty Council had twenty-four full voting student members.

While many professors and administrators had originally faced the prospect of student participation with some trepidation, it is now generally agreed that students are making valuable contributions to decision-making. There still is, and probably always will be, some small amount of friction, but in general student involvement has proceeded smoothly. There have been none of the bitter words and political in-fighting that greeted similar transformations in the Faculty of Arts and Science. In Engineering the two 'estates' found themselves able to work together in a spirit of co-operation.

The end of the sixties was a turbulent time for student government in general at the University of Toronto. Student organizations were on the whole moving from a social to a much more political emphasis; there were continual cries for greater student representation on the university's decision-making bodies. The Students' Administrative Council epitomized the expanded political activity of student governments – especially in the Faculty of Arts and Science. With a half-million dollar budget and a relatively small number of committed people, the SAC worked hard but with limited success to politicize the student body. It often tended to give one-sided, and sometimes extremist, representations of student opinion.

To the credit of the Engineering Society and engineering students, they did not shrink from becoming involved in student politics at the university level, even with the demanding course loads that most of them had. Some held executive positions in the Students' Administrative Council and some were elected to the new Governing Council of the university. In many ways, the Engineers acted as a moderating force, and a powerful one, when the rhetoric of student *politicos* became too heated or distorted. With the help of the Medsmen, they often provided an effective counterbalance to displays of radicalism on the part of some of the politicians at the SAC.

One of the most important such occasions took place in the fall of 1969 during the so-called 'discipline crisis.' The Students' Administrative Council had called a mass student meeting in Convocation Hall and had invited President Claude Bissell to attend with the aim of embarassing him publicly. Over a quarter of the students in Engineering, some six hundred strong, skipped their classes to show up early and occupy all the choice front-row seats. A packed house greeted Bissell when he entered to give a short address; the Engineers then led everyone present in a standing ovation for the president. In sharp contrast was the sight of thirty or so student *politicos* sitting at the corner of the stage, looking disgruntled and dismayed.

This incident also highlighted one of the most colourful faculty members of the time, Professor W.F. Graydon, head of Chemical Engineering. Bill Graydon was continually urging his students to get involved in the affairs of the university; when the exodus to Convocation Hall came, it was he who led the Chemical Engineers, or 'Graydon's Raiders' as they were more popularly known, on the march. His chauvinistic attitude towards his department created a tremendous *esprit de corps* amongst the boys in Chemical. He had quite a reputation as a lecturer too; Graydon could postulate and expound upon a world philosophy based solely on the three laws of thermodynamics.

Professor Graydon and his Engineers in many ways symbolize the growing fervour, among staff and students, to revitalize the educational system surrounding them. Because the student of the seventies is personally involved in the planning of his curriculum, and because he is committed to the banishment of social ills, he is in general more highly motivated to work for himself. His energy has turned largely from fun-filled antics to what he feels are more fruitful pursuits.

Although many problems have developed as side effects of the multiple changes taking place in the early seventies, prospects seemed to have brightened since the sixties. At all levels Engineering has moved forward rapidly: students, teaching staff, and administrators have co-operated in joint evolution. This firm foundation and unity allows all the members of the Faculty to look with confidence towards the future.

The academic staff

When James Watson Bain, the second head of the department of Chemical Engineering, was awarded an honorary LL D in 1948 by his own university, the citation read as follows (the emphasis is mine):

The traditions from which a university draws its surest strength are largely shaped, neither by the antiquity of its foundation nor by the modernity of its equipment, but by the character and calibre of its staff, by *teachers* who are both *creative scholars* and *inspired preceptors*. Of this noble company is James Watson Bain, for over half a century member and head of the Department of Chemical Engineering in this university, a man whose powers and vision have continued to grow with the passage of the years. To him the duties and challenges of his profession extend far *beyond the confines of lecture hall and laboratory*: to students about to enter upon a career, he is a *wise and generous friend*; to associates in the field of chemical engineering, he is a leader whom they have delighted to honour; to his fellow-citizens, he is *a wise and valued counsellor* in many worthy enterprises.

These words sum up much of the spirit of these pages devoted to the academic staff in Applied Science and Engineering, for they touch upon every important area of faculty activity; the key words and phrases indicated in italic have been chosen as principal themes for what follows.

The citation begins with a reference to teachers, and teaching has always been the common denominator, the foundation, of staff activity. From the study in depth of a subject demanded of a teacher if he is to organize and teach it effectively as an 'inspired preceptor' spring naturally the investigation and the research that are the hallmarks of the 'creative scholar.' Yet students may often look to their professors for more than teaching. Among the staff have been many whose devotion to students, as counsellors, as 'wise and generous friends,' has made them the beloved and trusted confidants of generations of students.

Through his role in helping to establish the first course in chemical engineering in a Canadian university, Bain provided an example of the vision and the creative thrust of the staff in changing the structures of the Faculty and the content of its programs to meet the everchanging needs of an increasingly technological society and of education for technological careers. The wider university as well has benefited from the dedication and drive of the members of the staff, for many have played leading roles outside the confines of Engineering itself. What also emerges over the past half century is the part the staff have played 'beyond the confines of the lecture hall and laboratory' as leaders in scientific and professional societies, as practitioners in their profession, as concerned citizens of the local community, as advisers to government, as emissaries to foreign countries.

The pages that follow contain numerous examples to justify such tributes. Unavoidably some past and present colleagues have received special attention while others have been left unmentioned. To do full justice even to the research work of the past twenty-five years would be a task quite beyond this volume. The individual accomplishments and honours that are mentioned are only examples; many others might equally well have been chosen. Hence a special tribute must be paid at the outset to those whose work has not been 'focused' in individual concrete accomplishments of the kind that, being highly 'visible,' lead to professional and public recognition. The character and spirit of our institution are in large part the integrated result of the efforts of many such teachers and scholars, who have rendered conscientious and dedicated service to their students, their faculty, their university, and their community year after year after year.

On the teaching staff of the Faculty in the session 1920-1 were forty persons having the rank of lecturer or higher. There were in addition thirty junior members – demonstrators, instructors, fellows. The distribution by rank of the senior members may be compared with that fifty years later (table 1). Although the total number increased during this half-century four and one-half times, the number of lecturers fell by nearly half. This reflects the current state of the academic market place: today new staff are normally PH DS appointed at the rank of assistant professor. The distribution by highest degree is further evidence of the shift in formal academic qualifications. In

TABLE 1

	1920–1	1970–1
Deans	1	2
Professors	9	52
Associate professors	9	68
Assistant professors	5	51
Lecturers	16	9
Total	40	182

1920 only one staff member had an earned doctorate, and only eight had master's degrees, a total of less than 25 per cent with advanced degrees. Another three had professional engineering degrees such as CE (Civil Engineer) or EE (Electrical Engineer). One had no university degree at all. In 1970, by contrast, 90 per cent of the staff held master's or doctor's degrees. The staff had also acquired a cosmopolitan flavour. In 1920 almost all were local products – graduates of the University of Toronto. In 1970, the place in which the highest degree was earned was distributed as follows: Toronto, 38%; elsewhere in Canada, 11%; USA, 24%; UK, 11%; Europe, 14%; other, 2%.

How did the teaching staff spend their time at either end of the half-century? A representative average teaching load in 1920 for the senior ranks was about nine hours of undergraduate lectures per week and responsibility for some laboratory work. In 1970 the comparable figures are about four undergraduate lecture hours, two hours of graduate lectures, and some responsibility for laboratory work. But while the 1970 professor spent less time in the classroom than did his 1920 counterpart, he was in addition most likely supervising three graduate students in project or thesis work for M ENG, M A SC, or PH D degrees. This is, of course, simply evidence of the growth of graduate work and research, a growth that has produced profound changes in the lives of Engineering professors. We have relatively scanty information about the publications of the staff in earlier days, about their lecturing activities outside the university, or about the honours they received, but now we have a fairly complete account in the list of scholarly addresses and publications published each year in the President's Report. For the typical year 1969-70, it lists thirty-four honours awarded, 209 scholarly addresses outside the university, and 304 publications. During that year there were as well two patents issued and eight patent applications filed by members of the Engineering staff.

INSPIRED PRECEPTORS

Although the recent waves of unrest among students the world over have had their effects at Toronto, and the relationship between teacher and student is already changing quite noticeably, the era we are writing about was for the most part 'traditional.' The teacher performed his function *vis-à-vis* undergraduates in the relatively formal context of the lecture room and the laboratory. As every student past and present well knows, there is a great variation in the lecturing style and ability of the staff, spanning the range from poor to superb. The majority of our teachers have fulfilled their lecturing duties with solid competence, delivering well-organized and well-prepared lectures. Of the few at the tail end of the distribution the less said the better. But every student who has passed through this Faculty has been exposed to at least a few outstanding teachers – great communicators, whose lectures were pertinent, well organized, interesting, and lucidly presented. Bringing their own enthusiasm for their subject into the classroom – an enthusiasm that in many cases miraculously survived year after year – they have kindled the interest of all but the most unresponsive of students.

Peter Gillespie, enthusiastic and fluent, made structural engineering a living subject for his students. He would often become so engrossed in his teaching that he would continue well past the hour. C.R. Young's lectures were examples of clear connective logic that always seemed to end with one of his hands on the door as the last word was spoken. The fame of Tommy Loudon as a teacher of statics had spread so widely among students that it came to the ears of this graduate even before he came to the campus as a student. Bobby Angus passed on his genius for hydraulics to a generation of graduates who went on to develop the hydraulic structures of the Ontario Hydro – T.H. Hogg, R.L. Hearn, Otto Holden, and J.J. Traill. R.F. Legget, who left to become head of the National Research Council's Building Research Division, and who received an honorary degree from the university in 1969, was known to students of the late thirties and the forties as the epitome of organization and lucidity. For sheer entertainment (and as a 'character') Morley Lazier probably had no peers during the forties. More recently Bill Graydon's exuberant and uninhibited style of lecturing – sometimes with musical accompaniment – has recaptured something of that quality. Pat Foley's lectures on 'Man as a Machine' and 'Man as an Information Processor' have been acclaimed by all attending them. On the laboratory side, P.B. Hughes will be remembered by hundreds of students for the meticulous and helpful commentaries he wrote in their lab reports. Alumni will no doubt recall many other teachers who left indelible impressions on them, who in one way or another struck that responsive chord that inspired them to learn. Although he was not a member of the Engineering staff, it would be injustice not to mention here John Satterly, a physicist who made an unparalleled impact on generations of students in Engineering Physics. Surely one of the greatest and most devoted of science teachers, he inspired, instructed, and entertained with wit, charm, insight, and an incredible array of lecture room demonstrations.

If the relationship of academic staff to undergraduates has been formal in the sense described above, a new dimension has been added with the development of graduate work. Graduate lectures are of course similar to undergraduates ones, although classes are usually smaller and there tends to be more direct student participation. The big change comes when the student is inducted into the research group of an individual professor, joining other graduates at various stages in their programs, and is assigned a thesis topic in the professor's current field of interest. In frequent one-to-one meetings, teacher and student discuss progress, identify problems, and decide how to proceed. Here the knowledge, experience, and enthusiasm of many a professor are seen at their best. Some who are quite undistinguished in the lecture room shine as supervisors. Those who have watched the transformation of a student from inexperienced apprentice at the beginning of the master's year to self-assured competence and mastery of his subject at the end of the PH D cannot help but feel a warm sense of accomplishment. This is the teaching process at its very best.

WISE AND GENEROUS FRIENDS

The life of a student in Engineering has never been easy. In the early twenties he had over thirty hours per week of assigned lectures and laboratories, and a heavy load of homework to boot. (The Faculty has since reduced the contact hours over the years by about one third for most programs.) Academic work has not been the only source of stress on students. There were in addition depressions in the twenties and thirties, war in the forties, and the bewildering pace of social and technological change in the fifties and sixties. Rare is the student who passed through his undergraduate and postgraduate years without experiencing problems –

academic, financial, vocational, emotional – that prompted him to turn for help to his teachers. Although the university in recent years has introduced central counselling and psychiatric services, the front line for Engineering students has always been the staff, who have almost without exception given guidance and counselling. What student in the thirties and forties did not know that if he were in trouble he would receive a sympathetic hearing from Bill Wright, who as professor of engineering drawing met most of them? To three decades of students in Engineering Physics, K.B. Jackson was adviser, counsellor, sympathetic ear, substitute father, and friend. No amount of trouble or personal sacrifice has proved too much for L.E. Jones (Mechanical Engineering) when he has perceived a student to be in need of his help. (Ted Jones' extracurricular services to students have also included his famous 'sliderule lectures,' and 'dissertation on dress and deportment' for the annual Graduation Ball.) The staff of the Faculty office as well has always carried a large burden of student counselling, and the sympathy and sage advice of Stewart Wilson, Jim Gow, and Bill Dowkes has always been valued by staff and students alike.

CREATIVE SCHOLARS

Knowledge is the medium in which the university professor practises his art. This art itself can be seen as having three parts. First, the professor adds dimensions of form and understanding to factual knowledge somewhat as a sculptor adds form to his clay; as Poincaré put it, 'A collection of facts is no more a science than a pile of bricks is a house.' Second, it is now widely accepted (although it was not always so – Cardinal Newman specifically rejected 'scientific and philosophical discovery' in his concept of a university) that a major aspect of the professor's work is to add to the store of human knowledge through investigation and research. And third, he communicates – to his students and to the world, through his lectures and his writings – the results of his intellectual efforts in organizing and understanding that which was already known, and in adding to it. The practice of this three-part art constitutes 'creative scholarship.' Some mention has already been made of the teaching role. Let us now turn to the areas of publication and research.

The writing of books primarily involves the organization and shaping into a coherent whole of substantial bodies of subject matter already known, although frequently new information resulting from the author's own research is included as well. The last half-century at Toronto was ushered in by several well-known books: R.W. Angus, first head of

Mechanical Engineering, published *Theory of Machines* (1917) and *Hydraulics for Engineers* (1929); E.A. Allcut, who succeeded Angus, wrote *Engineering Inspection* (1922), and C.R. Young produced *The Principles of Specification and Agreement Writing* (1931). These have been followed by some twenty-five additional books written alone or with colleagues by Allcut (two more), B. Chalmers, D.J. Clough, R.S. Cobbold, B. Etkin (two), I.I. Glass, J.G. Hall, J.M. Ham, F.C. Hooper, M.W. Huggins, P.B. Hughes, G.N.J. Kani, S. Kotz (two), R.F. Legget, R. Luus, I. McCausland, N. Moody, C.F. Morrison, G.N. Patterson (two), A. Porter (two), G.R. Slemon, I.W. Smith, and Young (eight more). The titles of the three most recently published illustrate some of the modern fields in which the staff are active: *Theory and Application of Field Effect Transistors* (1970) by Cobbold, *Kinetic Theory of Gas Flows* (1971) by Patterson, and *Dynamics of Atmospheric Flight* (1972) by Etkin.

In keeping with the intensification of research activity in the last two decades, the number of published papers and reports – the immediate fruit of such research – has increased enormously. A large majority of the current staff has a significant publication record. Among the more prolific are Howard Rapson (Chemical Engineering) with 75 papers and 23 patents, H.S. Ribner (Aerospace Studies) with 70 papers, S.N. Flengas (Metallurgy and Materials Science) with 64 papers, Norman Moody (Biomedical Electronics and Engineering) with 38 papers and 36 patents, and E.J. Davison (Electrical Engineering) with 61 papers.

Most of these publications are the outcome of the professors' own research and that of their graduate students. The extent of study is dramatically illustrated by the 1970 progress report of the Institute for Aerospace Studies (UTIAS), which lists 134 separate projects and investigations financially supported by twenty-one different agencies outside the university, including both industry and government in Canada and the United States: brief descriptions of these projects occupy 204 pages of text and illustrations. Since UTIAS and its sister Institute of Biomedical Electronics are structural elements of the Faculty devoted primarily to research and graduate study, their emphasis on research might be expected to be higher than in the undergraduate teaching departments. All the latter have nevertheless made substantial contributions. For example, Mechanical Engineering listed eighty-five projects in its 1969 annual report.

Such a volume of research defies comprehensive description within a few pages. The few examples which follow have been chosen rather arbitrarily: they fail to include the greater part of the staff's significant work. Perhaps some future historian will undertake the monumental task of describing it in full. It is hoped, however, that they do give the correct flavour – that they show something of the scope and quality of this profes-sorial activity, which unfortunately is that least understood and least appreciated by the general public.

Mining
Among the earliest research accomplishments were those of H.E.T. Haul-tain. His work in industry before he joined the staff had shown him the need for proper analysis in the ore-dressing industry, so important to Canada, of sub-sieve particles. His subsequent inventions as a member of the staff – the superpanner and the infrasizer – have been widely used the world over. Not only did he invent and develop them, but he personally super-vised their manufacture and testing.

Hydro-electric power
In the pioneering days of this new energy form in Ontario, as its use spread from lighting to electric motors, a new and pressing need developed – to control the frequency (i.e., generator speed) under conditions of fluctua-tion load and variable hydraulic head. That electric clocks keep such good time, and that synchronous motors run with such constant speed, is largely due to the pioneering efforts of H.W. Price (the second head of Electrical Engineering) who with G.F. Tracy and C.K. Duff developed an ingenious speed-regulation device based on a pendulum clock and an intricate combi-nation of cams and switches. Price received the McCharles Prize for this work; Tracy later succeeded Price as department head; and Duff became the Hydro's leading specialist in frequency control.

Synthetic rubber
In a number of cases, engineers have joined the Faculty after establishing themselves as creative researchers elsewhere. One such was R.T. Woodhams who was appointed to Chemical Engineering in 1968, and whose field is high-polymer chemistry. While manager of chemical research at the Dunlop Research Centre in Sheridan Park, Ontario, he was co-inventor of an elastomer (synthetic rubber) that has become since 1960 the world's second largest rubber in production. His current research is in the area of reinforced plastics, particularly composites involving mica flakes (a material of which Canada has reserves of several billion tons). These materials may ultimately replace metals in many structural and mechanical applications.

Rocket probes
To obtain information about the composition and processes of the outer reaches of the atmosphere (above 70 km) is an essential part of the search

for a fuller understanding of the atmospheric envelope that blankets the earth. At the Institute for Aerospace Studies, J.H. De Leeuw and his graduate students have made substantial contributions to upper-atmospheric research with a series of probes launched by Canadian-built Black Brant rockets from Fort Churchill. The rocket nose cones, and the instrumentation and telemetry equipment with which they are packed, were largely designed and built by De Leeuw and his group. Among the equipment is a novel electron beam probe which has been successfully used to obtain the first direct measurements of the air temperature at this high altitude. This technique has since been adopted by other researchers.

Metallurgy

Professor Karl Aust, of Metallurgy and Materials Science, has for some years been studying the properties of lead. In recent research he has obtained new insights into the process of surface hardening, discovering that surface strength depends on oxygen and impurity content. This highly significant fundamental work was recognized in 1971 by the Hofmann Memorial Prize – an award made only once every three years by an international tribunal of experts in metallurgy and lead technology.

Quasars

Among the most puzzling of astronomical objects are quasars. These faintly visible stellar-like spots in the sky emit strong radiation in the radio-frequency range. A team of National Research Council and university scientists, including Alan Yen of Electrical Engineering, was the first to succeed in measuring the diameters of quasars using long-baseline radio interferometry. The system used two radio telescopes at bases in Penticton, BC, and Algonquin Park, Ontario, 1,900 miles apart, with two synchronized atomic clocks as time references. Yen and his co-workers were awarded the Rumford Medal of the American Association for the Advancement of Science in 1971 for this achievement.

Internal combustion engines

Members of Mechanical Engineering, beginning in 1947, carried out an intensive study of the process of combustion in internal combusion engines. The project was led by R.O. King, who had come to the Faculty from the Defence Research Board, assisted by A.B. Allan, Sam Sandler, and Bill Wallace. This group succeeded in producing controlled combustion of hydrogen in an engine cylinder, and later produced much vital detailed information about the combustion processes in hydrogen and liquid-fuelled engines. From their work has grown the current graduate research program on exhaust emissions from automobile engines.

Surgical adhesives
For thousands of years, the only method available to surgeons for closing incisions and joining biological tissues has been the suture. Although adequate for many applications, it is a crude legacy of the past, not at all in harmony with the sophistication of other aspects of modern surgical procedures. In consequence there has been an intensive search during the past decade or so for a satisfactory biological adhesive that could replace stitching. Foremost among the researchers in this field is P.Y. Wang, of the Institute of Bio-Medical Electronics and Engineering, who with E. Llewellyn Thomas (a qualified physician as well as an engineer) has made a major advance through the development of a rapid-setting polyurethane adhesive that is flexible and well tolerated by tissues. Their fundamental research on the mechanisms of bioadhesion have shown them how many common glues might be converted into useful surgical adhesives. This recent discovery offers the potential for great improvements in surgical therapy.

Glued-laminated timber beams
A significant innovation of the Canadian construction industry following the second world war was the development and introduction into service of the aesthetically pleasing glued-laminated timber beam, in highway bridges, buildings, and other structures. Although the actual safety performance of these beams was very good, structural engineers grew seriously concerned as partial delaminations were observed in a number of installations. Professor Mark Huggins, aided by a team of undergraduate and graduate students, carried out a study of the extent, cause, and effect of this phenomenon. Through millions of cycles of repeated loadings on specimens in the laboratories of Civil Engineering, they simulated heavy service conditions on highway bridges. As a result, the load-carrying capacity and life expectancy of these beams can now be predicted with a high degree of accuracy. Huggins, and two of his students, E.N. Aplin and J.H.L. Palmer, were awarded the Gzowski Medal of the Engineering Institute of Canada for their papers on this subject.

BEYOND THE CONFINES OF THE LECTURE HALL

Some of the activities of Engineering professors reach far beyond the lecture room, the laboratory, or the library. These begin close at home, in the academic committee room and the Faculty Council chamber, for the duties of teaching staff have always included policy-making and administration related to their department, faculty and university. The process of curricular and structural change has increasingly involved standing and special committees. Among the most important in recent years have been the Committee on Development, 1955-6, chaired by Ross Lord; the Faculty Study Committee, 1961-4, chaired by Jim Ham; the Special Committee on Curriculum, 1968-9, chaired by Ben Etkin; the Faculty Structure Committee, 1969-70, chaired by Cameron Kenney, and its successor in 1970-2, chaired by Olev Trass.

The innovative thrust of the staff in the evolution of the Faculty is nowhere better illustrated than in the founding and building of new structural units. Gordon Patterson was architect and builder of the world-renowned Institute for Aerospace Studies, inaugurated in 1949; Arthur Porter was the founder and first head of Industrial Engineering in 1961; Norman Moody provided the inspiration and leadership for the interdisciplinary interfaculty Institute of Biomedical Electronics and Engineering created in 1962.

The staff have over the years shared also the responsibility for the development and operation of the university as a whole. Some have played leading roles in the University of Toronto Faculty Association: Ham, Rapson, Etkin, Alec Collins, R.W. Missen, M.R. Piggott, and S.J. Uzumeri have all represented the Faculty on that body, and several have served as executive officers or committee chairmen. At another all-university level, engineers have served on the President's Council and the Central Budget Committee (Rapson, Etkin), on the Commission on University Government (Etkin), on the University-Wide Committee (Burke, Uzumeri, Charles), on the Committee on Discipline (Ham), the Committee on Supplementary Income and Related Activities (Ham, Missen), and on the Library Council (Slemon, Cobbold). Mike Piggott was chairman of the Presidential Advisory Committee on the Social Responsibilities of the University, and Morris Wayman served as chairman of the Innis College Council. For several years following his retirement in 1966, R.R. McLaughlin continued to serve his university; first as chairman of the Presidential Advisory Committee on Accommodations and Facilities (PACAF) and then as chairman of the Planning Division. Other members of the staff have been prominently involved in university-wide athletics, drama, and music.

This community mindedness has spread beyond the campus into local social, political, and religious activities. To choose but three from many examples: Professor Haultain was founder of the Technical Service Council, and originated and carried through an extensive program of occupational therapy in Ontario hospitals for disabled veterans of the first world war. R.W. Angus rendered such outstanding service to the Yorkminster Baptist Church that he was honoured in 1928 by a special presentation. W.F. Graydon was three times elected to the Etobicoke School Board, and was twice its chairman.

If Engineering staff have been concerned and active in the communities in which they live, they have been even more so in the wider community of those who share their professional and scientific interests. The record is replete with examples of staff members who have played leading roles in national and international professional organizations. Again a few random examples: R.R. McLaughlin was a founding member and first president of the Chemical Institute of Canada; Ben Bernholtz and John Abrams have both held positions of leadership in the Canadian Operational Research Society; Gordon Patterson has been president of the Canadian Aeronautics and Space Institute; C.R. Young was president of the EIC, and Mark Huggins has been chairman of its Bridge and Structural Division; Fred Rimrott, Doug Baines, Jim Keffer, and Ian Currie have played leading roles in the International Union of Theoretical and Applied Mechanics and in the organization of the Canadian Congresses of Applied Mechanics; Don Allan was instrumental in the formation of the Canadian Society of Mechanical Engineers; Ben Alcock is a commissioner of the International Union of Pure and Applied Chemistry.

When foreign universities have turned to Toronto's Engineering Faculty for help, it has responded in full measure. In 1961 Dean McLaughlin toured India to assist in the establishment and operation of engineering colleges there: the sequel, which saw seven professors follow to carry on with this project, has been told in an earlier chapter. In 1971 Gordon Slemon went to the University of Havana to help the engineering staff there in the development of a master's program. Subsequently a visit of several of the Cuban staff to Toronto initiated a program of further visits by members of the Faculty to Havana to provide teaching and leadership in areas where that university remains deficient. A similar program has provided assistance to the University of the West Indies in Jamaica.

Assistance has also gone to universities closer to home. Arthur Porter (Industrial) served as academic commissioner to the University of Western Ontario, producing a comprehensive analysis of its entire academic structure and recommendations for future change; Bill Winegard (Metallurgy) left to assume the presidency of the University of Guelph; A.I. Johnson (Chemical) has become dean of engineering at Western, and a number of other former staff members are on the faculties of other Canadian and foreign universities.

Many of the staff have made important contributions to policy as advisers to governmental and other bodies. E.A. Allcut was a founding member of the Ontario Fuel Board in 1956 and was much concerned with atmospheric pollution from thermal power plants. (The current wave of public concern about the environment has had many notable precursors among engineers and scientists.) Ross Lord was instrumental in developing the flood control plan for the Toronto region in 1954, and was the second chairman of the Metropolitan Toronto and Region Conservation Authority; during his tenure this body quickly moved beyond a narrow interpretation of its role to build a remarkable system of recreational resources. Ralph Rice served on two Provincial commissions concerned with the mining industry. Bob Jervis, having advised the Canadian government of the danger of mercury pollution as early as 1966, subsequently established the first Canadian program for monitoring mercury levels. Pat Foley has served as the representative of Canada on the NATO Human Factors Advisory Group. G.W. Heinke has advised the Department of Indian Affairs and Northern Development on problems of the Arctic environment. H.S. Ribner has been chairman of the Sonic Boom Panel of the International Civil Aviation Organization (ICAO). Arthur Porter was chairman of the Advisory Committee for Science and Medicine for Expo 67 in Montreal. A large number of the staff have served on the grants committees and associate committees of the NRC and DRB as members and as chairmen. Jim Ham has been a member of the NRC and was the first chairman of the Committee on Engineering Education of the World Federation of Engineering Societies. Especially noteworthy in the policy field is Gordon Patterson's two terms of office on the highest body for science policy in Canada, the Science Council.

This section on outside activities would be incomplete without some observations related to professional practice by the staff. An engineering school can be credible only if it has on its staff a large number, preferably a large majority, of members who have had significant practical experience. Engineering professors at Toronto have a long tradition of direct professional service to industry and the community. Until the end of the forties this often took the form of summer employment, although private practice flourished as well. In the last two decades the growth of graduate studies and research has substantially changed this pattern; research is now a year-round activity and professors are rarely free to take summer jobs.

Many examples exist of engineering work accomplished by the staff.

Haultain (at the age of 21!) designed the world's first electric mine hoist in Europe in 1890. Lloyd Pidgeon invented and developed the 'Pidgeon process' for the production of metallic magnesium and served widely as a consultant to the metallurgical industry. Howard Rapson, with patents in forty-three countries, has through his consulting activities been a major influence on the pulp and paper industry in Canada and elsewhere. Arthur Porter, during six years with Ferranti Electric in Toronto, pioneered the use of modular units and printed circuits in computers. The design of the hydraulic works of the Ontario Hydro on the Niagara and Ottawa rivers were dependent upon model studies carried out in the Mechanical Building under the direction of Ross Lord, Ted Jones, and Grant Huber (who later joined the staff of McMaster). The tallest building in the Commonwealth was, until about 1967, the Bank of Commerce building on King Street in Toronto; T.R. Loudon was one of the designers of the structure of this and of many other buildings, including Varsity Arena and Stadium. Carson Morrison, Charlie Hershfield, Mark Huggins, and Laurie Kennedy (who left to go to Carleton) have been associated with the designs of a wide range of structures including microwave towers, bridges, the Stratford Festival Theatre, and the Canada and Ontario pavilions at Expo 67.

Obviously a first-rate engineering school represents a collection of talents, expertise, and facilities unlikely to be duplicated in any industrial or governmental establishment. Access to this pool will inevitably be sought by outside individuals or organizations with technical problems they want solved (and professors thus are often in the position of acting as consultants to consultants). Indeed, one might be suspicious of the quality of a faculty not so sought after. Society cannot afford, nor should it wish, to deny those who need it the use of these resources. To have teaching staff, and sometimes students, involved solving 'real-world' engineering and scientific problems is of benefit to all concerned. The client gets a solution to a problem or the answer to a question, the staff and students gain experience and some extra remuneration. The curricula, both undergraduate and graduate, are influenced for the better, and much new and worthwhile research is inspired. In the changing pattern of professional activity, the near-elimination of summer work has been accompanied by a growth in consortia of staff organized to provide professional services. Two of these, involving staff in Civil Engineering, operate as normal commercial organizations outside the university, with the university personnel associated in a part-time role. Others, in Electrical Engineering, Chemical Engineering, and the Institute for Aerospace Studies, operate somewhat more loosely and do not have outside facilities or personnel.

The range of professional services that have been provided by faculty members is wide. It includes analysis, design, testing in special facilities, and advice and support to small companies developing their own engineering and research capabilities. The Chemical Engineering group alone has helped some twenty small companies start new research projects with NRC funding. The Aerospace group has done important work for Canadian industry and government and for NASA in the USA. This group, together with colleagues in Mechanical Engineering, have been pioneers in the field of architectural aerodynamics. The final shape and structure of Toronto's City Hall were based on tests carried out in the wind tunnel of the Aerospace Institute. The Electrical Engineering group has rendered valuable service to the power, electronic, and computer industries, both in Canada and abroad, and has worked closely with the Ontario government to assist smaller companies that need engineering advice.

Finally reference should be made to the 'spin-off' companies that have come into existence as a direct result of research and invention by faculty members. Sinclair Radio Laboratories Ltd, with branches in Ontario, New York State, and Australia, is the best known example – a company that has pioneered in the field of specialized antenna design and manufacture. Vehicle Research Ltd, in which members of Electrical Engineering are involved, is a spin-off of the clean air car race in 1970 in which 'Miss Purity,' the University of Toronto entry, distinguished itself. It is now in the process of developing a low-pollution automobile for the commercial market.

In this chapter I have attempted to convey to the reader some feeling for the character and the activities of the teaching staff of the Faculty of Applied Science and Engineering. In so doing I have chosen staff functions and staff activities as the central theme and have brought in particular individuals primarily by way of illustration – chosen to some extent at random. The result is that many colleagues and friends, senior and junior, past and present, are not mentioned at all – J. Roy Cockburn, A.R. Zimmer, Bob Wiren, W.M. Treadgold, Bill Sagar ... Paul Biringer, Peter Wright, Frank Hooper, Irv Smith, Jack Breckenridge, George Craig, Earle Burke – a list simply too long to complete. I can only express my profound regret that I have been unable to write about the personalities and accomplishments of all of them, men who, in the words of my opening quotation, by their 'character and calibre' have shaped and are now shaping 'the traditions from which a university draws its surest strength.'

PHILIP A. LAPP

The nation builders

'Five ... four ... three ... two ... one ... lift off!' – and Canada entered the space age, as the massive Thor-Agena rocket lifted the nation's first satellite into orbit to send back data about telecommunications in our far north. In the control centre in Ottawa on that late September day in 1962 was Andy Malozzi, a 1953 graduate of School, a key member of the design team that had worked for over three years on Alouette.

Exactly eighty years earlier, in the fall of 1882, a civil engineer freshly graduated from School found himself sloshing through muskeg north of Lake Superior. He was running levels for what turned out to be the most difficult section of the new Canadian Pacific Railway that linked the Dominion coast-to-coast. From there James H. Kennedy, the third graduate of SPS, went on to become one of Canada's most eminent pioneer railway construction men.

These two circumstances symbolize the contribution of University of Toronto engineers over eight decades to the building of Canada, for since Confederation transportation and communications have provided the physical bonds that unite this vast land into a single nation. Engineering in all its forms, moreover, has played a central role in the material development of Canada. Yet, as we shall see, Schoolmen have accomplished far more than the design and construction of artifacts. After graduation, they have tended to diffuse rapidly throughout the labour force – the majority in leadership roles. They are to be found in business, industry, and commerce, performing supervisory, planning, and executive functions. Engineers have managed and controlled the physical development of

TABLE 1

University of Toronto engineering graduates by program

Program	First graduates	Last graduates	Total number of diplomas and B A SC degrees[1] granted to 1971
Civil	1881		3,582
Mining	1886	1967	939
Mechanical[2]	1890		3,777
Analytical and Applied Chemistry	1890	1920	66
Architecture	1892	1947	222
Chemical	1905		2,831
Electrical	1911		3,159
Metallurgy and Ceramics	1916		579
Geology	1939		248
Engineering Physics, Engineering Science, and Aeronautical	1938		1,538
Engineering Business and Industrial	1948		1,103
			18,044

1 Three-year diplomas were granted up till the spring of 1911. Thereafter the Faculty granted only four-year diplomas, the first being granted in 1913. There was no class of 1912.
2 Mechanical and Electrical diploma program up to 1911.

Canada, for better or for worse: this chapter will attempt to reveal the breadth and depth of the accomplishments of Toronto's graduates in this process.

In connection with its hundredth anniversary, the Faculty of Applied Science and Engineering, together with the Engineering Alumni Association, commissioned a career profile study of each graduate whose address was known. The purpose was to gain a better understanding of how careers develop from graduation, how the organizational structures within which engineers work are changing, and how Toronto graduate engineers disperse throughout the economy and labour force. The study will be used by the Faculty in the design of future curricula, and it will guide counsellors in advising young people on engineering career alternatives. It also should be useful to manpower planners in developing a closer match between the supply and the demand for various categories of engineers. Only the highlights will be covered here; the main report has been published separately and is available from the Faculty.

TABLE 2

Professional Engineers graduated in Applied Science and
Engineering from the University of Toronto (as listed in
the *Directory of Professional Engineers of Ontario*, 1971)

Category	Professional engineers	Percentage of total
Industry	4,810	55.5
Education	627	7.6
Construction	190	2.2
Municipal	240	2.8
Consulting	1,000	11.5
Government	902	10.3
Utilities	580	6.7
Retired	300	3.4

Since its first graduate in 1881, the Faculty had awarded a total of 18,044 diplomas and bachelor degrees up to December 1971. Table 1 shows their distribution by program. Of these, approximately 16,000 are still alive – 6,300 in Metropolitan Toronto, 5,700 in other communities throughout Ontario, 2,000 in other provinces of Canada, 1,500 in the United States, and close to 600 in other areas of the world, on all continents. Up to 1971, there had been 82 women graduates. The 1971 registry of the Association of Professional Engineers of Ontario listed 8,649 Toronto graduates. Their occupational categories are shown in table 2.

The career profile questionnaire was mailed to 13,540 alumni during May 1972. By mid-summer, replies were received from over 4,100 persons – a return of 30 per cent, and a good sampling from most years over the past forty. Some of the more salient results are illustrated in figures 1 to 5.

Figure 1 shows how rapidly engineers move into supervisory and senior positions after graduation. As expected, most graduates started in non-supervisory, technical jobs, but within ten years over two-thirds moved into supervisory, management, or executive positions. Within twenty-five years of graduating, 60 per cent were in either management or executive roles, and nearly one-third have ultimately reached the executive ranks.

Figure 2 indicates how many graduates practise in the branch or field of engineering they studied at university. About 40 per cent have not continued within their chosen branch even immediately after graduation. Within twenty-five years, apparently less than half were still practising in their original field of study, and at least one in seven had left engineering practice entirely.

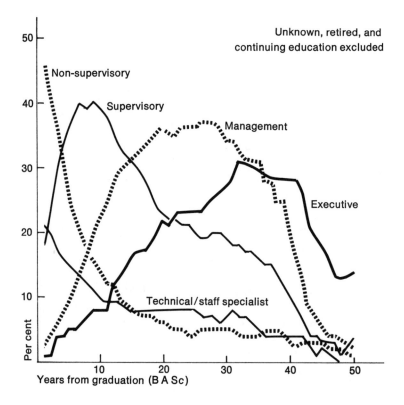

Figure 1
Changes in the distribution of engineers (B A SC only) according to management role

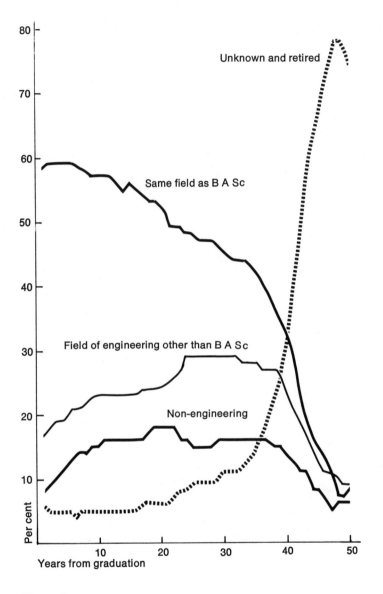

Figure 2
Changes in the field of engineering since graduation (B A SC)

Figure 3
Distribution of the stock of University of Toronto engineering graduates each year
according to sector of the economy

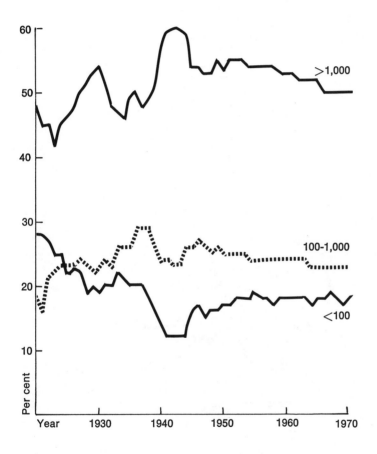

Figure 4
Yearly distribution of University of Toronto engineering graduates according to size of company

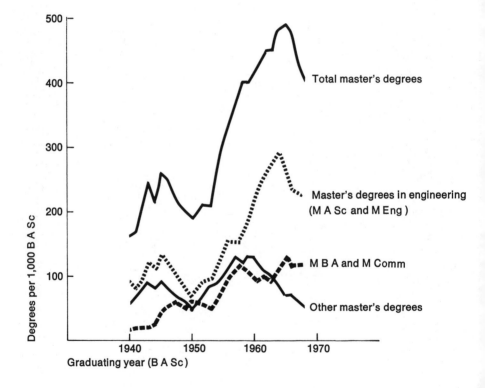

Figure 5
Master's degrees per 1,000 graduates by year of graduation smoothed over 5-year
intervals

Figure 3 reveals the rapid decline in the number of engineers in the secondary manufacturing industries. These include firms making durable and non-durable goods and in construction, which have been employing fewer and fewer engineers since the mid-fifties. In the same period, more engineers have been finding jobs in the tertiary or service sector which includes consulting, education, government, utilities, communications, transportation, finance and business, and personal or community services. Resource extraction has employed fewer engineers since the late thirties, reflecting increased automation and efficiency. Figure 3 suggests that Canada is indeed moving towards a post-industrial society.

Figure 4 shows the distribution of Toronto graduate engineers in relation to the size of their organizations. Clearly the majority have found work in large operations – one half of them in companies with more than 1,000 employees, and about 75 per cent in companies with over 100. The pattern has not changed significantly over the years, which is remarkable when contrasted with figure 3. It can only be concluded that the larger organizations are the dominant users of engineers, regardless of their sector of the economy.

Figure 5 illustrates the massive trend towards graduate studies that has occurred since the mid-fifties. The curves show the number of graduate degrees ultimately acquired (as of 1972) by members of each graduating class. In recent years, up to 25 per cent of the graduating classes have moved directly into graduate work either at Toronto or another university (not shown on any of the figures), and ultimately *half* the recent classes have earned master's degrees. The likely reason for the tail-off after the mid-sixties is that many graduates are still studying for advanced degrees. The trend of the curves suggests that even higher percentages can be expected over the next few years, at least until graduate enrolments level off across Canada. Approximately 60 per cent of the master's degrees are in engineering and 20 per cent in business, with the balance in various branches of science.

In summary, the survey has shown that engineers diffuse rapidly throughout the labour force in positions of responsibility; many leave their original branch of specialization and some leave the field entirely. While most graduates tend to be employed by the larger organizations, there is a swing from manufacturing and construction towards the service industries. Since the second world war, increasing numbers of engineers have felt that there are advantages in acquiring an advanced degree and have returned to university as full- or part-time graduate students, usually within eight to ten years after graduation – approximately 40 per cent of them in fields other than engineering.

Many graduates who have been out of School more than ten or fifteen years would admit that they either have forgotten or have not used much of the material they absorbed in their undergraduate years – particularly those who moved into semi- or non-technical occupations. While this may be the case, their careers usually started in a technical capacity. The essence of engineering is design, and design involves quantitative decision making. The engineering curriculum has been structured to develop this capability in the individual, and those who also have acquired the necessary communication skills usually move into supervisory or management positions.

The task of documenting the achievements of over 18,000 graduates is quite impossible in any reasonably finite span of time. Even if such information were available, it would be equally impossible to condense it into a few pages. The university's Graduate Records Office maintains files on the career progress of thousands of University of Toronto alumni gleaned from newspaper clippings, articles, and press releases. The files on several hundred engineering graduates are contained in this collection, and they became the starting point in the research for this chapter. Libraries, newspaper morgues, telephone conversations, and personal interviews were used to uncover further information that resulted in a file of over eight hundred names of graduates whose accomplishments could be identified. Lists of honours and awards, *Who's Who* listings, and the Canadian engineering societies provided further help in identifying individuals and the significance of various achievements.

In spite of all of this research, I am acutely aware that many significant contributions have been omitted. Furthermore, it has not been possible to acknowledge even all of those on the short list of eight hundred names in what is to follow. The intention is to portray the contribution of Toronto's graduate engineers to the development of Canada as a nation, in the hope that it will instil a deeper sense of pride in the institution where Schoolmen learned their skills. To those who have been omitted – apologies. Engineering is a social or team activity and few engineers stand alone in their achievements. The success of any one is most often symbolic of the efforts of many others.

We begin again with the railroads.

The railroads epitomize early team activity in building Canada; it is fitting that Toronto's first engineering graduate, James L. Morris, spent the five years immediately after graduation in construction work with the CPR in the foothills of the Rockies and later in northern Ontario. Later, after opening private practice in Pembroke, Ontario, he became an authority on drainage work and, among other engineering achievements, laid out the townsite of Sudbury. Unlike most succeeding Schoolmen, he was active in local politics, serving as mayor of Pembroke for several terms. Later he became chief engineer and inspector of surveys in the Ontario Department of Lands and Forests – a role that provided him with a wealth of material for future publications. He was the author of *Indians of Ontario,* an official history published by his department, and, after retiring in 1943, he wrote historical articles concerning various Ontario centres and was associated with the preparation of a history of Algonquin Park.

Engineer, politician, administrator, historian – as the first graduate Morris set a challenging pace for the engineers who have left Varsity since. He entered SPS almost by accident. When he first came to Toronto from the upper Ottawa Valley, he tried to enrol in University College, but found that in the course he wished to enter there were no special lectures and drafting rooms. The registrar told him, 'You'd better cross the lot to that red brick building where they're starting up a School of Science.' In 1927, the university conferred on him the honorary degree of Doctor of Engineering.

Following Morris and J.H. Kennedy, many early graduates contributed to the building of Canada's two railroads. J.M.R. Fairbairn, '93, joined the CPR in 1899; when he retired after twenty years as chief engineer in 1938, he had played a major part in extending the mileage from 8,500 to over 17,000 miles. W.A. Duff designed and built railway bridges from his graduation in 1901 until he retired from the CNR as engineer of bridges and roadways in 1932. On special assignment, he was responsible for the restoration of railways and dock terminals after the Halifax disaster of 1917. F.V. Seibert, '09, after a distinguished career as explorer and surveyor in the west and northwest for the federal Department of the Interior, was engaged by the CNR in 1929 as superintendent of natural resources and development and later, in 1940, as industrial commissioner – a position he held until retirement in 1950.

Toronto's tenth engineering graduate rose to railroad distinction in the United States. A.R. Raymer, '84, became chief engineer and later assistant vice-president of the Pittsburgh and Lake Erie Railroad and of the Lake Erie and Eastern Railroad. He also was a director of nine subsidiary railroads and president of four of them.

The spread of the iron rails was synonymous with the early development of Canada, but today the railroad has been all but replaced by the airplane as the main form of travel. Canada, motivated by its vast size and long distances, has always been a world leader in aviation, beginning with the earliest history of flight.

On 30 January 1911, J.A.D. McCurdy, '07, almost – but not quite – flew to Havana. He was out to win $8,000 in prizes offered by Cuban interests for the first aviator to complete the hop from Key West, Florida. After a long wait for good weather, he finally got away at 7:30 am. He wore an ordinary business suit and took his seat in the Silver Dart as calmly as anyone getting ready for an automobile trip. But within ten miles of his destination, his oil ran out and he was forced down into the ocean. The plane touched down so perfectly that he was not even splashed. The machine was dragged aboard a destroyer and that afternoon McCurdy went aloft in Havana and raised the Cubans' hair with the first aerial stunts they had ever seen – an effort so striking that all the prizes were presented to him despite his failure.

McCurdy accounted for many aviation 'firsts.' He made the first flight over British territory, the first inter-city flight between Toronto and Hamilton (in a record time for the distance of thirty-six minutes), the first figure-eight in the air, and the first flight in Mexico; he transmitted the first wireless message from a plane in 1911, and flew the world's first flying boat in 1914 – truly a remarkable record.

It all started in Baddeck, Nova Scotia, where he was born and where Alexander Graham Bell had established a summer home. Bell knew McCurdy as a boy and followed his development with affectionate interest. In the fall of 1903, McCurdy was sent to study engineering at the University of Toronto where he met and formed a lasting friendship with F.W. (Casey) Baldwin, '06, grandson of Robert Baldwin, the Upper Canadian statesman. After graduation, McCurdy returned to Baddeck and invited Casey for a summer vacation. He stayed forty years.

With Bell, the two young engineers, together with Glenn Curtis and Lieut Thomas Selfridge of the u.s. Army, in 1907 formed the Aerial Experiment Association of Baddeck. This group built several experimental aircraft, leading up to the Silver Dart biplane which incorporated 'ailerons' and a tricycle landing gear. It had a 50-horsepower engine which drove a pusher propellor about eight feet in diameter.

On 23 February 1909, only twenty-one months after leaving School, McCurdy piloted the Silver Dart over the ice of Baddeck Bay for a distance of about a half mile and at a height of some thirty feet. It was the first flight over British territory.

Eleven months earlier, Baldwin had flown the Red Wing, designed by the same group, at Lake Keuka, NY. It was the first *public* flight in North America (the Wright brothers' work in 1903 having been carried out secretly), and Baldwin was the first British subject and the seventh person ever to fly.

After two hundred subsequent flights of the Silver Dart at Baddeck, McCurdy and Baldwin took the machine to Petawawa Camp where they demonstrated four successful flights to the Canadian Army with both aboard. On the fifth, the aircraft crashed and the military concluded that the airplane had no use in warfare; the tests were dropped.

At the outbreak of war in 1914, McCurdy approached Sam Hughes, then defence minister, with the idea of organizing a Canadian flying force. Hughes rejected the airplane as 'an invention of the devil' that 'will never play any part in modern warfare,' but later he changed his tune. In 1915 McCurdy organized the Curtis Aviation School at Toronto Island which trained over six hundred pilots without a fatal accident, including the famed ace, Raymond Collishaw. Then he turned his attention to the newly formed Curtis Airplane and Motors Ltd in Toronto where he produced some two thousand Flying Jenny fighter planes. In 1928 he founded the Reid Aircraft Company and developed Curtis-Reid Flying Services Ltd with himself as president, a post he left at the outbreak of the second world war to serve as director of purchases in the Aircraft Production Branch of the Munitions Department and later as special assistant to the department's financial adviser. Finally, in 1949, he was appointed lieutenant governor of his native province, Nova Scotia, and served in that post for six years before retiring from public service.

Another graduate of the same era as McCurdy and Baldwin, T.R. Loudon, '05, was an aviation pioneer in his own field – education. As head of the Department of Civil Engineering after 1943, he revitalized the program in aeronautical engineering at the University of Toronto. During the second world war he commanded the RCAF Test and Development Establishment.

Many Toronto graduates who followed made further important contributions to Canadian aviation. John H. Parkin, '11, initiated, designed, and installed a four-foot wind tunnel for aerodynamic research at the University of Toronto in 1917. During the next twelve years, with this facility he helped to design the Vedette, Varuna, and Vista flying boats used for forest patrol and fire fighting, the Velos for aerial surveying, and the Vanessa for mail and passenger service – all for Canadian Vickers Ltd in Montreal. All this was done in his spare time and during summer vacations: his laboratory was not yet recognized as an integral part of the University. (In 1910, when Parkin had selected 'The Aeroplane' for his graduation thesis, the subject was rejected as not being scientific; only after some persistence was it eventually accepted.) Only in 1928 did aeronautics finally gain academic recognition, when Parkin initiated the first aeronautical engineering program in Canada. He left the university in 1929 to continue his aeronautical research at the National Research Council, and became the first director of the National Aeronautical Establishment in 1951.

When Parkin left Toronto, the course in aeronautical engineering was temporarily abandoned. Two of his former undergraduate students, however, went on to fame – B.S. Shenstone, '28, and J.T. Dyment, '29. His research in aerodynamics was carried on at Toronto by Professor Loudon and a graduate student, Gordon Patterson, who later became founding director of the university's Institute for Aerospace Studies, a position he still holds.

Toronto-born Bev Shenstone acquired his fame abroad. On Parkin's advice, after graduate studies he went to Germany for practical experience and there worked with Alexander Lippisch, the famous Messerschmitt designer. Later he went to England to join the Supermarine Aviation Company, where he collaborated with Reginald J. Mitchell in the design of the Spitfire, and was responsible for its highly successful aerodynamic performance. After serving with the British Ministry of Aircraft Production and as a technical aide to C.D. Howe, he was appointed chief engineer of British European Airways in 1948 and in 1960 was appointed a member of its board.

The story of Jack Dyment is synonymous with the history of Air Canada. When in 1938 he joined Trans Canada Air Lines, as the company was then called, its fleet consisted of a few Lockheed 14s and Electras. Through a progression of improved aircraft – the Lodestar, Lancastrian, DC-3, North Star, and Super-Constellation, into the turbine fleet of Viscounts and Vanguards, and on to the pure-jet DC-8, DC-9, and 747 – he provided a guiding hand as chief engineer. Concurrently he built up the firm's engineering organization, methods, and facilities to a point where Air Canada is now one of the world's largest and most reliable lines. Dyment received many distictions – among them the presidency in 1964 of the Society of Automotive Engineers, the first non-resident of the United States to hold that office.

In the early years of the second world war, Toronto-trained research engineers made important contributions to flying equipment. J.K.W. Ferguson, '36, co-developed the rubber oxygen mask which superseded the U.S. mask used in the 1930s, and J. Shortreed, '27, co-invented a portable oxygen tank which, attached to a heated flying suit, made possible high-altitude bail-outs.

In 1943, another Parkin protégé, Kenneth F. Tupper, '29, was sent by the National Research Council on a mission to England so secret that not even his superior knew the reason. He was the first Canadian civilian to learn of Britain's plans for jet aircraft. It had been recommended that stands be built near Winnipeg to test the jet engines developed by Frank Whittle, under extreme low temperatures comparable to those that would be met at high altitudes. During the next two years, Tupper was chief engineer of the Crown company, Turbo Research Ltd, which was created to conduct the tests and build a team to develop jet engines in Canada. The company was subsequently taken over by A.V. Roe Ltd.

After the war, Tupper switched into the Atomic Energy Division of the National Research Council and became director of engineering responsible for the start-up and operation of Canada's first nuclear reactor – the NRX. As the result of a chance meeting with Sidney Smith, then president of the University of Toronto, in an Ottawa-Toronto parlour car, he became dean of the Faculty in 1949 – a post he left in 1954 to become a consultant until he was recalled to the NRC as a vice-president in 1964.

A.V. Roe Ltd owed its early success in the design and manufacture of jet engines to two graduates of the Class of 1939 – Paul B. Dilworth and Winnett Boyd. Dilworth, as manager and chief engineer of the Gas Turbine Division, and Boyd, as chief designer, were responsible for Canada's first jet engine, the Chinook. Like Tupper, both went on to make important contributions in nuclear power and established themselves in the consulting field. The Gas Turbine Division later became Orenda Ltd, which has become a major world supplier of jet engines and components under the engineering leadership of B.A. Avery, '46.

Another member of the Class of 1939, John L. Orr, working at the NRC in 1945, developed a method of ice and frost removal from aircraft parts that is being used by many major airlines and has contributed significantly to flight safety and efficiency. Orr went on to design many government programs of industrial assistance as science adviser to the minister of industry, trade and commerce, and later as Canada's first scientific attaché in London for the Ministry of State for Science and Technology. Carrying on NRC's pioneering work in aeronautics today are, notably, R.J. Templin, '44, in aerodynamics, and E.P. Cockshutt, '50, in jet engine technology.

The top student in the Class of 1950, one of the largest in School's history, was W.R. Laidlaw, son of Justice R.E. Laidlaw, a 1915 graduate of School. He headed the proposal team that won the multi-billion dollar Apollo contract for North American Aviation, in which firm he rose to be vice-president. Later he was called to the Pentagon to test the highly controversial F-111 swing-wing fighter, and then established his own company in Newport Beach, California. Laidlaw started his career as a designer with the famous de Havilland Aircraft of Canada engineering team on the Otter aircraft.

That de Havilland team, led by R.D. Hiscocks, '38, (now an NRC vice-president), was responsible for the design of the Chipmunk, Beaver, Otter, Caribou, Buffalo, and Twin Otter series. The simplicity and sound engineering of these rugged aircraft have won them a market in over sixty countries. Some of the Toronto engineering graduates responsible for this success have been W.T. Heaslip,'47, now vice-president engineering, J.P. Uffen, '44, R.G. Batch, '51, R.B. McIntyre, '36, W.H. Jackson, '39, R.E. Klein, '42, G.W. Johnston, '48, plus the two Jackson brothers – G.R., '54, and G.B. '56 – sons of Professor K.B. Jackson, '16, who founded the Engineering Physics program and directed it until he retired in 1966.

Bush aircraft accelerated the development of Canada's natural resources, carrying prospectors into districts which would not otherwise have been explored for many years. Aircraft also flew in with drilling equipment, and when cores flown out seemed to show promise, it was aircraft that transported men and tools to the site.

Exploration and surveying are necessary precursors to resource discovery and exploitation. Toronto graduates contributed significantly to the early opening of Canada's frontiers, as well as to later development. School's seventh graduate, James W. Tyrrell, '83, conducted the first exploratory survey of the country between Great Slave Lake and Hudson Bay in 1900. Among the top surveyors to graduate from School was A.J. Campbell, '05, who between 1912 and 1924 mapped the mountain peaks along the British Columbia-Alberta interprovincial border by pioneer work in the use of phototopography. In the 1940s he surveyed the British Columbia-Yukon boundary along the sixtieth parallel, running his line as high as 6,400 feet, mostly in bad weather.

Such early exploration and surveys paved the way for those who were to probe and exploit Canada's great mineral wealth. Varsity produced many leaders in the mining field, but few as versatile as Eldon L. Brown, '22, whose skill in such diverse fields as exploration, research, development, mining, milling, refining, and finance guided the growth of Sherritt Gordon Mines from its inception in 1922. After Brown was hired as superintendent to develop the northern Manitoba mine, aircraft were used for the first time to transport diamond drilling equipment to the site.

The development of the Lynn Lake nickel operation in Saskatchewan was also a story of Eldon L. Brown, who there had to apply his earlier experience at Sherridon on a much larger scale. One of his early moves, in 1949, was to engage Frank A. Forward, '24, a professor at the University of British Columbia, to find a better way to extract nickel from the Lynn Lake ore. From his long experience in nickel refining in Japan and Cuba, Forward worked out a radical new process of leaching the ore with chemicals instead of smelting it with heat. This work in hydrometallurgy culminated in the construction of the Sherritt refinery complex at Fort Saskatchewan. Forward later became the first director of the Canadian government's Science Secretariat, established in 1964 to shape a science policy for Canada. Despite serious financial crises, Brown brought the refinery into profitable operation using the lowest grade nickel deposits in the Western world.

Another giant resource extraction industry, Cominco, also owes much of its success to Toronto-trained engineers. The hiring of R.W. Diamond, '13, was the turning point in the fortunes of this company, which in 1910 had purchased the Sullivan property and its complex lead, zinc, iron, sulphide ore. Initially the lode was mined for lead, but during the first world war an urgent demand for zinc developed and the government asked Cominco to undertake its production. This proved a costly process until Diamond, who had previously worked on the flotation process in the United States, applied the technique for Cominco. Finely ground ore in water was treated with one reagent and then subjected to air agitation. The lead accumulated in the froth and was skimmed off. A second reagent was introduced, air applied again, and this time the zinc floated off. By 1923, after changes and refinements, the process was incorporated in a new plant at Kimberley, BC. Cominco had till this time been a company which could make money only when metal prices were favourable. With differential flotation, it was assured a long life and an annual income measured in millions of dollars. After heading up the concentration department, Diamond was put in charge of the fertilizer production program and was largely responsible for the giant plant at Trail, BC. A recipient of many honours, he later became the company's general manager.

Following closely in Diamond's footsteps was William S. Kirkpatrick, who joined Cominco immediately after graduating in 1926 as a metallurgical engineer. He was co-inventor of the sulphur recovery process, developed at Trail in the early 1930s, which reduced the damage to vegetation from expanding metal production in the area. The recovered sulphur was consumed in large quantities by the fertilizer plant. Kirkpatrick rose in the company to succeed Diamond as assistant general manager in 1945. Fourteen years later he was named president, and in 1966 became chairman and chief executive officer.

Another Schoolman, H.R. Banks, '14, made his mark at Cominco's Sullivan mill by making possible the economic recovery of its tin. The rapidly expanding mass of tailings contained this metal at a concentration of only 0.055 per cent. Using gravity separation techniques, Banks initiated Canada's first tin production to meet wartime needs.

Many Toronto engineering graduates have risen to the top of the Canadian mining and metals industry. R.A. Bryce, '04, arrived in Cobalt, Ontario in 1907, the same year the railroad opened it up as the first mining town of any consequence in Canada. He became superintendent and later manager of the Silver Queen and Beaver mines, but was best known as president and managing director of Macassa Mines – a property in the Kirkland Lake area that he acquired after leaving Cobalt. He served on the Board of Governors of the University of Toronto for twenty-four years and was named president of the Canadian Chamber of Commerce in 1949.

The most famous mine at Kirkland Lake probably was the Lake Shore. There J.C. Adamson, '24, served for thirty years as chief engineer and superintendent, retiring in 1961 as vice-president operations.

The life of Morson S. (Pop) Fotheringham, '31, stretches as a continuous thread through the history of Steep Rock Iron Mines. He moved to that mine in 1938 at the age of 29, with a new bride, to set up shop in a log cabin and conduct a drilling program. Then he contrived one of the boldest strokes of engineering in the history of mining on this continent – to divert the water and drain the lakes which covered the ore. It has been estimated that the iron deposits exceed a billion tons. Fotheringham progressed to president and general manager of the company in 1950.

Another graduate, James D. Cumming, '08, holds nearly fifty patents on mining equipment and gear for the armed forces. He is also the author of the *Diamond Drill Handbook,* and, on the lighter side, his column 'Now and Then' delighted readers of *The Northern Miner* for a dozen years. There are many other names that deserve mention in this area. A method for the direct reduction of iron ores to steel was one of several patents held by Patrick E. Cavanagh, '37, working with the Steel Company of Canada. One of Canada's best-known metallurgists, he later became president of Premium Iron Ores Ltd. The use of carefully sized pellets of ore in grinding mills instead of steel balls was developed by B.S. Crocker, '32, and his associates. A few of the other graduates who have made it to the top in the mining and metals industry are Marsh A. Cooper, '35, president of McIntyre Porcupine Mines Ltd, and later president of Falconbridge Nickel Mines Ltd; Fraser W. Bruce, '25, president of the Aluminum Company of Canada; Frederick J.E. Lockhart, '41, president of Noranda Manufacturing Ltd, and his classmate W.A. Robinson, president of Newconex Holdings Ltd.

Toronto-trained engineers also have taken part in framing the regulations that have governed resource extraction. In northern Ontario, George R. Mickle, '88, Toronto's first professor of mining, helped the provincial government to draft the Ontario Mines Act and Ontario Mines Tax Act. In 1907, he was called from the university to serve as Ontario's first mine assessor, and became a world-recognized authority on mining taxation.

Following a similar pattern, J.T. Cawley, '43, resigned in 1950 as head of the Mining Department of Ontario's Lakehead Technical Institute to become director of mineral resources in the Saskatchewan Department of Natural Resources, later becoming deputy minister. In this position, he has become known internationally as a resource expert – particularly in oil – and has served overseas as a United Nations adviser in Burma and Indonesia.

The oil industry, like mining, has benefited from Toronto's engineering alumni. Canada's western oil boom in the early 1950s was sparked by Imperial Oil's successful drilling at Leduc, Alberta. The man behind that achievement was John R. White, '31. He became president of Imperial Oil in 1953 – at 45 one of the youngest presidents of any major company in Canada at that time. Later he was appointed a vice-president of Standard Oil of New Jersey, the largest oil company in the world. Other prominent oilmen from School have been K.F. Heddon, '33, president of the Sun Oil Co, H.B. Keenleyside, '23, president of an oil company bearing his own name, and J.W. Kerr, '37, president of Trans-Canada Pipelines.

While the development of Canada's mineral wealth was an important factor in building the nation, the management and exploitation of our renewable resources has been no less significant. The pulp and paper industry and its suppliers has grown to become one of Canada's major exporters, and it is not surprising that, as in other fields, Toronto engineer alumni played a major role. Eli Cowan, '23, inventor of the Cowan screen and several other machines for pulp and paper processing, established a firm with his brother, Ben Cowan, '32, that designed paper mills for all parts of the world. C.A. Sankey, '27, of the Ontario Paper Co, in Thorold, Ontario, co-developed the first commercially feasible formation tester, which gives an automatic analysis of the fibre clot structure, thus providing for improved quality control at higher web speeds.

Elliott M. Little, '25, started at Abitibi as an office boy at Iroquois Falls in 1914, and worked his way up the ladder to the top of the pulp and paper industry. He took electrical engineering following first world war service in the RAF, then returned to Abitibi and rose to assistant manager. In 1932 he joined the Anglo-Canadian Pulp and Paper Mills Ltd at Quebec City and in nine months was appointed general superintendent. During the second world war, Little headed the National Selective Service of Canada, in control of the country's manpower. After the war he returned to Anglo-Canadian and in 1958 became chairman of the board after thirteen years as the company's first Canadian president.

Other Toronto engineering graduates who rose to senior positions in the pulp and paper industry have been F.S. Seaborne, '23, president of Kimberley Clark; R.A. Irwin, '31, president of Bathurst Power and Paper; W.H. Palm, '33, executive vice-president of the West Virginia Pulp and Paper Co; and K. Patrick, '36, manager of research and development of the Fraser Companies.

Canada's other major renewable resource is its water, and here too many Schoolmen have achieved distinction in the management and control of this increasingly scarce commodity. Alberta owes the transformation of its dry southern regions into farmland to P.M. Sauder, '04, 'Mr Irrigation,' who came to southern Alberta in 1909 in charge of the federal government's hydrometric surveys in the west, and saw the potential that lay in the land. In 1920 he joined the Lethbridge Northern Irrigation District and watched a dustbed, where 75,000 acres of wheat had blown out of the ground, develop into a garden spot where close to a thousand farm families found an assured and comfortable living. Sauder helped solve problems of colonization and settlement as well as of engineering. He also worked on many other irrigation schemes in Alberta, and served as director of water resources from 1940 to 1944, during which time he outlined plans for irrigation implemented after the war.

The man who organized the federal hydrometric survey was J.B. Challies, '03. As chief hydraulic engineer of the Department of the Interior and director of water power and reclamation, he supervised basic water resource surveys and general power studies covering Canada's principal rivers. He was also a consultant on matters relating to international waterways for the Department of External Affairs. He left the government in 1924 to join the Shawinigan Water and Power Company, retiring as senior vice-president in 1952. Challies was succeeeded in his federal post by J.T. Johnston, '10, who had developed a system of water resource inventory which was subsequently adopted by all the provincial power and water administering organizations.

When the St Lawrence Seaway Authority ultimately came into being, another Toronto man, R.J. Burnside, '27, a canal engineer on the Trent and the Welland, was appointed director of operations and maintenance.

The construction of the famous hydraulic lift-locks on the Trent Canal was the work of Walter J. Francis, '93, who also designed the Don siphon for the main sewers in Toronto.

One of the top sanitary engineers on this continent, A.E. Berry, '17, studied public health after graduation. As the director of sanitary engineering for Ontario's Health Department, he effected the complete chlorination of all the province's surface water supplies and reduced the typhoid fever rate to Canada's lowest. The compulsory pasteurization of milk in the province was largely due to his efforts. When the Ontario Water Resources Commission was formed in 1956, he was appointed its first general manager and chief engineer. The first two chairmen of the OWRC also were Schoolmen – A.M. Snider, '17, and J.A. Vance, who studied civil engineering from 1911 to 1914. A sanitary engineer of more recent vintage, Lorne Van Luven, '48, has been outstanding as a member of international committees on effluent control, and in bringing continuously high rate activated sludge treatment to North America.

Another Schoolman who contributed significantly to the management of Canada's water resources was Professor George B. Langford, '23, a mining geologist in the Department of Geology. He established the Great Lakes Institute at the university and was its first director. In other fields, he was largely responsible for the establishment of an engineering technicians' program in Ontario, assisted in the creation of the Ontario Securities Commission, helped provide the framework for the former Ontario Planning and Development Department, and was the first man to undertake scientific studies of the Great Lakes system in Canada.

Across the border, A. Ralph Thompson, '36, directs the Rhode Island Water Resources Center.

The economic exploitation of our natural resources and the subsequent development and growth of our manufacturing industries originally was made possible by tapping the energy potential of Canada's waterways. The harnessing of these mighty and powerful rivers, surveyed and catalogued by such people as Challies and Johnston, is once again largely a story of Toronto engineering graduates.

When Sir Adam Beck, father of the Ontario system, toured the province arguing for publicly owned power distribution, the man who stood beside him with facts and figures was F.A. Gaby, '03. He served as chief engineer – Ontario Hydro's principal executive officer – from 1912 to 1934.

A classmate of Gaby, H.G. Acres, was in charge of a general water power survey of Ontario which laid the foundation for the vast service network of Ontario Hydro. As chief hydraulic engineer, he supervised and placed into operation the world's first 55,000-horsepower turbine at the Queenston-Chippewa development in 1921. During his career, he directed the design and construction of power installations totalling more than 1,000,000-horsepower in generating capacity. In 1924, he formed a consulting firm bearing his own name that has grown to be one of the largest in Canada.

Gaby and Acres, while still in their twenties, collaborated on the new transmission line from Niagara to Toronto. In the protests made by financial critics of the provincial government, there was scathing denunciation of the 'young whippersnappers, just out of college, who dared to say that the line could be built for $3,500,000 when Toronto's leading banker knew that even $12,000,000 was insufficient!' Adam Beck staked his reputation on the professional judgment of his young engineers. The project was completed for only $3,350,000 – in spite of towers and insulators overdesigned to quiet the apprehensions of those inhabiting the route, and an inflated cost of right-of-way.

This line established the validity of Canadian innovation in electrical technology and gave a great impetus to the evolving power grid. More than six decades later, Canada is still the world's leader in high-voltage transmission.

T.H. Hogg, '07, succeeded Acres and rose to become chairman and chief engineer of Ontario Hydro in 1937. An international authority on hydro-electric design and development, he provided consulting advice to the provinces of Manitoba, Saskatchewan, and Alberta and, after retirement, served on the team that was responsible for the St Lawrence Seaway development. When he was chairman, his executive assistant was Richard L. Hearn, '13, who later also became chairman. A former chief engineer of H.G. Acres and Company, Hearn was loaned during the war to the Polymer Corporation in Sarnia to supervise the construction of its synthetic rubber plant. In 1952, to mark his service to Ontario Hydro and his capabilities as an engineer, the largest fossil fuel power plant built in Canada to that time was named after him – the Richard L. Hearn Generating Station at Toronto.

Other Hydro developments named after Schoolmen have been the J. Clark Keith Generating Station at Windsor and the George W. Rayner Generating Station on the Mississagi River. Keith was a member of the Class of 1910, Rayner of 1905.

One October morning in 1915, a classmate of Hearn was shivering as he jotted down water levels at Ontario's new Eugenia Generating Station. But when his notes dropped into the icy tail-race, he just gritted his teeth and plunged in after them. On 1 July 1958, that same engineer, Otto Holden, pressed a button, and set in train the highpoint in his 47-year career with Ontario Hydro. The button set off a charge that blew up the coffer dam that loosed the water which was to create the new Lake St Lawrence and put into operation the St Lawrence power and seaway project. It was a dramatic moment, not only because of the size and importance of the work, or because Holden had first made a drawing for the project in 1919, but also because the exact date of the button-pushing had been set four years before when the first sod was turned. The ceremony marked a perfection of timing. By this time Holden had succeeded Hearn as chief engineer. Over the years he was connected with some of Hydro's biggest developments including all the Ottawa River projects, Sir Adam Beck Generating Stations No. 1 and No. 2, and the St Lawrence Seaway project.

The seaway marked the last major hydro-electric development in southern Ontario, and while coal plants were already in use, the discovery of the world's largest uranium field in Ontario's Blind River-Elliott Lake region in 1953 opened vast new possibilities for power development. Hearn saw the potential of nuclear power for Ontario Hydro and, as chairman, made an agreement with Atomic Energy of Canada Ltd for collaborative design and construction of nuclear power plants. Harold A. Smith, '41, was sent to Chalk River to take charge of Ontario Hydro's team there. Smith conceived the idea of using pressure tubes, instead of the massive pressure vessels employed by the Americans and Europeans, to contain the coolant within the reactor. His concept was incorporated in the CANDU line of reactors which now is beginning to receive world attention owing mainly to the recent success of the Pickering nuclear generating station – 2,000 megawatts capacity when all four units come into operation. Today Smith is Hydro's chief engineer, at the helm at a time when new sources must be tapped to meet a provincial appetite for power that is doubling every ten years. At AECL a recent graduate, George Pon, '50, heads the design team for Power Projects as general manager–engineering.

Lack of a reliable supply of heavy water has become one of the major obstacles to the future use of the CANDU nuclear reactor. Failure of the heavy water plant at Glace Bay, NS, has been a centre of controversy and concern. An interesting twist of fate is that Smith's brother, Walter, '42, heads the Canatom group charged with the onerous task of rehabilitating the Glace Bay Plant and bringing it into operation.

Other graduates who have made important contributions to Ontario Hydro include J.J. Traill, '05, responsible for the hydraulic design of most of Hydro's plants between 1927 and 1952, including the tunnels and canals for Sir Adam Beck Generating Station No. 2 at Niagara; W.P. Dobson, '10, director of research for many years; A.H. Frampton, '25, who played a leading role in planning and developing the frequency conversion plan for southern Ontario and later became general manager of the English Electric Company of Canada; C. Kent Duff, '18, an authority and pioneer in load-frequency control; and Gordon M. McHenry, '40, the present director of labour relations.

Outside Ontario Hydro, other Toronto engineering graduates have made their mark in the power field. One of the earliest was J.M. Robertson, '93, who developed the electric power industry in Cobalt in 1909. R.A. Ross, '90, the third chairman of NRC, designed plants in Canada, the USA, Asia, Europe, and Australia. Max V. Sauer, '01, worked with Acres on the Queenston-Chippewa project, and later was the hydraulic engineer responsible for the design of the Beauharnois power development on the St Lawrence River. A.W.F. McQueen, '23, was hired by H.G. Acres in 1929 and rose to become president and later chairman of that company. Under his stewardship, Acres undertook power projects in Jamaica, Ghana, Greece, Iran, Ceylon, New Zealand, and Pakistan, where it was responsible for the huge Warsak hydro-electric project employing 156 Canadians and 10,000 Pakistanis. A classmate of McQueen, Alexander Murray, inspired hydro-electric developments in Costa Rica by forming an international consortium to establish bauxite mining and aluminum refining in that country. Others who made it to the senior ranks have been C.N. Simpson, '15, general manager of the Gatineau Power Company, and W.M. Hogg, '39, president of the Great Lakes Power Corporation.

Few Schoolmen can boast of becoming a chieftain of an Indian tribe, but G. Herrick Duggan, '83, earned the title of 'Strong Iron,' the English translation of the name the Iroquois bestowed upon him. Duggan, School's sixth graduate, was at the forefront of Toronto graduates responsible for major engineering works in the construction of bridges, harbours, factories, buildings, and skyscrapers that have altered the face of Canada. His most distinguished work was the design of the Quebec bridge, hailed as an engineering wonder after two attempts to complete it had ended in disaster. For seventeen years Duggan was president of the Dominion Bridge Company. He was also a keen sailor who designed and built over a hundred yachts, won the Seawankaka Cup, and defended that trophy on nine occasions.

Col William George Swan, '05, was another of the breed – builder of bridges, moulder of skylines and shorelines. Founder of the consulting firm of Swan, Wooster Engineering in Vancouver, he was responsible for the Lion's Gate bridge, the Second Narrows bridge, the Tsawwassen ferry terminal, the Patullo bridge, the Kelowna bridge, Kitimat, and about 40 per cent of the piers, elevators, and other water-front structures built in the Vancouver area, all accomplished before he retired from the firm in 1967.

Another, A.H. Harkness, '95, accounted for some of Canada's biggest buildings – among them the Parliament Buildings in Ottawa; the Canadian Bank of Commerce in Toronto, tallest building in the Commonwealth at the time; the Sun Life building in Montreal, the Commonwealth's biggest office building at the time; and several other Toronto structures including the east block of the Ontario Parliament buildings and Toronto Western Hospital. As a hobby, Harkness turned his powers to gardening. Hundreds of people each spring and summer visited his extensive iris beds, in which he created new varieties, and brought other types to perfection.

Many other Toronto engineering graduates contributed to the building of their city. Two from the Class of 1906, A.E.K. Bunnell and E.L. Cousins, worked on the Bloor Street viaduct and the grade separation on the waterfront. Later Bunnell chaired the Metropolitan Area Committee which ultimately led to the creation of what is today the Municipality of Metropolitan Toronto. Frank E. Wellwood, '25, became Toronto's chief building inspector; R.L. Clarke, '37, became Metro's commissioner of works, and Sam Cass, '49, is Metro's roads commissioner. The new Toronto zoo is being prepared under the guiding hand of David H. Scott, '50.

The Angus family has roots deeply planted both in the Faculty and in the building of Toronto. The son of a self-educated mechanical engineer, Professor R.W. Angus, '94, served the university for forty-four years and was hailed as a pioneer in the study of water flow and hydraulics. His brother, H.H. Angus, '03, who was hired by George Westinghouse in the United States after graduation, returned to Canada to form an engineering firm bearing his name; this firm has been responsible for the mechanical and electrical work on many Toronto buildings including the Toronto General Hospital, Central Technical School, the central heating plant for the downtown hospitals, and the Toronto-Dominion Centre. His son, Donald L. Angus, '41, carries on the business.

Another family company, Frid Construction Co Ltd, has been responsible for major buildings in Hamilton, Ontario, one of the largest being the Hamilton Theatre Auditorium. D.K. Frid, '50, now is president, following his father, H.P. Frid, '11, who also served in key posts on the board of McMaster University during its years of rapid expansion.

The first superhighway in North America – the Queen Elizabeth Way connecting Toronto and Hamilton – owed its distinguishing features to Arthur Sedgwick, '09, who conceived the idea of the cloverleaf and designed the monument marking the eastern entrance. The first bridge on the four-lane highway was designed by C.C. Parker, '29, who later took on more exotic projects, including the port-works in Abu Dhabi on the Arabian Gulf.

Other Schoolmen headed south of the border to work in the field of construction. The twelfth graduate, E.W. Stern, '84, designed and supervised the construction of many important buildings in New York City before becoming Manhattan's chief engineer of highways. Bridges and buildings were the specialty of one of the famous Tyrrell brothers, Henry Grattan Tyrrell,'86, among them the bridge and tunnel connecting Norfolk and Portsmouth in Virginia, and the Château Frontenac hotel in Quebec City. Tyrrell, the author of eight volumes on engineering and architecture, also invented the automatic drawbridge gate and regulating gates for canals and waterways.

One of Tyrrell's classmates, T. Kennard Thomson, was considered in his day one of the world's greatest consulting engineers, and proved to be one of Toronto's most imaginative graduates. (As an undergraduate, he was founder of the Engineering Society.) One of Thomson's schemes was a six-mile extension of Manhattan Island, half a mile wide, south from the Battery. He also proposed a two million horsepower hydro-electric development at a dam four miles downstream from Niagara Falls, and a National Forest Park, twenty miles wide and fifteen hundred miles long, from Lake Superior to the Pacific, to provide forests, utilize farms too poor for agriculture, and form the world's greatest game preserve. Among his actual achievements were the invention of the pneumatic caisson and the designs of over thirty New York skyscrapers, including the famous Singer Building.

As in other fields, many Schoolmen have made it to the executive ranks in building and construction. They include C.R. Redfern, '09, president of Redfern Construction; R.E. Chadwick, '06, organizer and former chairman of the Foundation Company of Canada, and his successor, F.G. Rutley, '11; M. McMurray, '39, president of Dominion Bridge, and that company's chief engineer, T. Dembie, '36; W.P. Pigott, '39, and J.J. Pigott, '40, of Pigott Construction Co (another family business); J.D. Wilson, '45, president of Avalon Construction Co, and a classmate, S.C. Cooper, president and general manager of C.A. Pitts General Contractor Ltd; G.R. Steed, '49, and D.R. Evans, '50, of Steed and Evans Ltd; and H. and J.M. Tanenbaum, '53 and '55 respectively, vice-presidents of yet another family enterprise, York Steel Construction Ltd, founded by their father.

Many Canadian buildings owe their architectural design as well as their engineering to Toronto graduates. While the School of Architecture broke away from the Faculty in 1948, the accomplishments of its graduates before then must be recognized along with those of wearers of the iron ring. Indeed, it was a Schoolman, H.H. Madill, '11, who, as head of the architecture school from 1934 to 1957, oversaw the transition to independence.

Among Toronto-trained architects was the first woman to graduate from a Canadian engineering school, Esther M. Hill, '20, who practised in Toronto, New York, Edmonton, and Victoria, specializing in town planning. Later she took up hand weaving, wrote a book on glove making, and became director of Hobbycraft Studios in Victoria.

George R. Gouinlock, '21, designed the Temple Building at Bay and Richmond Streets in Toronto, the highest office building in the Commonwealth at the time, and twelve of the buildings of the Canadian National Exhibition. G.S. Adamson, '28, designed the first solar house in Toronto, the Hobbs Sun House on Dale Avenue, the Defence Research Medical Laboratories at Downsview, and the offices for Dow Chemical and the Polymer Corporation in Sarnia.

As head of one of the best-known architectural firms in Canada, John B. Parkin, '35, has well over a thousand buildings to his credit; two outstanding examples are the Toronto International Airport terminal 1 and, jointly with the Finnish architect Viljo Revell, the new Toronto City Hall. Another elegant structure, the Stratford Festival Theatre, which won the Massey Gold Medal for design, was the work of C.F. Rounthwaite, '42, and R.C. Fairfield, '43.

The physical development of Canada has depended not only on buildings and massive engineering works but also on less concrete achievements – notably in communications, which in the past half-century have replaced transportation as the national binding force. As might be expected, Toronto engineering alumni have played their part in this development. One of the key achievements in early radio was made by a Schoolman who left before graduating because he 'already knew more than his professors' about wireless and electronics.

In 1914, when he was fourteen years old, Edward S. (Ted) Rogers had already built his first receiving apparatus. Radios in those days were powered by a maze of storage batteries and dry cells which were expensive, bulky, unreliable, and continually running down. Rogers decided the batteries must go. He set to work inventing a new type of tube that could be run on alternating current, without the hum that had plagued all other such attempts and interfered with the signal. By 1925 he had filed his patent and set up the Rogers Majestic Corporation in Toronto to manufacture the Rogers batteryless radio. Then he turned to the more difficult problem of high-power transmitters, and in 1927 brought into operation the world's first batteryless broadcasting station, 9RB, which later became CFRB, today the largest privately owned station in Canada. The call letters commemorate his initial achievement – the CF stands for Canada, the RB for 'Rogers Batteryless.'

Schoolmen also contributed to the early development of television. In the late 1920s, C.F. Jenkins, '20, demonstrated the transmission of a picture by means of electrical signals using a Nipkow disc scanner. W.B. Whalley, '32, is credited with co-developing the original Orthicon tube used in TV cameras when he was with RCA in New Jersey during the late 1930s. The second world war brought Whalley back to Canada, where he developed the first operational radar in North America and used it to guard Halifax harbour at night. Later, he was responsible for creating the Tube Division of Research Enterprises Ltd in Leaside. After returning to RCA at Princeton, he developed the first UHF transmitters installed atop the Empire State Building.

The co-inventor of the first electrical gramophone pick-up device, Horace O. Merriman, '10, made an historic recording of the ceremony in Westminster Abbey which honoured the Unknown Soldier on 11 November 1920. A prodigious inventor, he pioneered work in Canada on radio interference with the armed forces and the Department of Transport.

When the United States was developing its ballistic missile early warning system, Jack E. Hogarth, '49, working at Canada's Defence Research Telecommunications Establishment, solved the problem of interpreting target return signals passing throught the ionosphere and the false alarms created by auroral phenomena. He designed and built the massive Millstone-type radar at Prince Albert, Saskatchewan, in the heart of Canada's auroral zone. The same antenna now is being used to receive signals from orbit carrying data on Canada's natural resources. A classmate of Hogarth, D.F. Parkhill, is the assistant deputy minister, planning, for the federal Department of Communications.

One of the builders of the extensive national and international services provided by the Canadian Broadcasting Corporation was R.D. Cahoon, '34. He joined the corporation when it was established in 1936, was appointed chief engineer in 1963, and later became vice-president, engineering. In the private sector, E.R. Jarmain, '30, has been associated with the growth of cable television in Canada as president of London Cable TV Limited.

Schoolmen also have made significant contributions to Canada's telephone system – one of the best in the world. The early work of A.S. Runciman, '11, of the Shawinigan Water and Power Co, in the 1920s paved the way for multiple communications on telephone lines strung along high tension live circuits. Such developments helped to make possible the Trans-Canada Telephone System, inaugurated in 1932.

R.J. Keefler graduated and joined Bell Canada as a commercial engineer in 1924. Over the next thirty-seven years he held several vice-presidential posts before moving to Bell's associate company, Northern Electric, in 1961 to become its president and later chairman. Other Bell Canada executives include J.V. Leworthy, '37, and W.R. Carruthers, '25. J.G. Little, '28, was vice-president for many years of Northern Electric. Another Toronto graduate, A. Brewer Hunt, '28, directed Northern's industrial research laboratories, the largest in Canada, through its period of major growth. Hunt was succeeded by Donald A. Chisholm, '49, who had previously made important contributions to the Apollo moon-landing program while on staff of the Bell Telephone Laboratories in the United States. In 1971, Bell Canada and Northern Electric established Bell-Northern Research at Shirley Bay near Ottawa with Chisholm as president.

Important as it is, such industrial research is only one ingredient needed for an expanding and healthy manufacturing industry. Sound management in all phases is the key to success in bringing new products and ideas to market.

Among the graduates of School's first century, one man emerged as an outstanding leader in the development and growth of Canadian manufacturing. He was Lieut-Col W. Eric Phillips, '14. After a distinguished army career in the first world war, he founded his own company in Oshawa, Ontario, selling mouldings, photo glass, and framed pictures. It grew to become Duplate Safety Glass Co of Canada, Ltd, with its products finding use across Canada in cars, trains, ships and airplanes, factories, and business offices.

During the second world war Phillips organized and was president of Research Enterprises Ltd, a Crown company set up to produce high-quality optical glass and precision instruments. Just before the war, he had founded Fiberglas Canada Ltd, which later turned its attention to new applications of its product in insulation, textiles, boats, and sports equipment. In 1949, he organized and became president and later chairman of Canadian Pittsburgh Industries, Ltd. He served as chairman of the giant

Argus Corp, and on the boards of other companies – two score of them at the time of his death in 1964.

In 1956, he was called in to take over the management of the ailing Massey-Ferguson Ltd as chairman and chief executive officer. In a matter of months he reorganized the company's worldwide operations and turned it around to the point where, in the year he died, it made $45 million net income. For nineteen years, from 1945 to 1964, he was chairman of the board of governors of the University of Toronto. It was his personal intervention that obtained for the university the abandoned munitions plant at Ajax as a postwar campus for the first two years of engineering. During his term as chairman, thirty-eight new buildings were constructed on the campus, a sister university (York) was sponsored, and plans were laid for two new suburban campuses – Scarborough and Erindale.

Phillips was an outstanding example of the large number of Toronto graduates who have moved into management and executive positions in secondary manufacturing industry. The extent of their numbers has been suggested in figures 1 and 3. Here, in a few paragraphs, it is impossible to portray even the breadth, let alone the depth of their achievements. Thus only an abbreviated listing of some who became the chief executive of their organization follows.

In the electrical and electronics industry, company presidents have included O.W. Titus, '17, Canada Wire and Cable; Carl A. Pollock, '26, Electrohome Ltd; Stuart D. Brownlee, '34, Canadian Admiral Co; Milton B. Hastings, '11, Powerlite Devices Ltd; H.A. Cooch, '09, and W.J. Cheesman, '43, both of Canadian Westinghouse. Peter Munk, '52, established Clairtone as a household word in hi-fi circles; now he is president of Pacific Hotels and Developments Ltd.

In the chemical industry, G.H.C.Smith, '32, became president of Bate Chemical Ltd, and D.C.R. Miller, '35, of Dow Corning Silicones. G.E.Willan, '41, became general manager of Niagara Brand Chemicals. R.J. Richardson, '50, is president of Dupont of Canada Ltd, and Gerald J. Ray, '49, president of the Borden Company Ltd.

C.J. Fensom, '03, son of the founder, was president of the Fensom Elevator Co. W.D. (Dolly) Black, '09, worked his way up the ranks to head the merged Otis-Fensom Elevator Co in 1935. Later W.J.W. Reid, '24, became president of the same company, and D.D. Panabaker,'33, its secretary-treasurer. M.C. Stafford, '21, was chairman of one of its competitors, Turnbull Elevator Canada Ltd; and Frank V. Reddy, '49, became president of the Dover Corporation (Canada) Ltd, Turnbull Elevator Division.

Fresh fruit, liquor, boats, forest machinery, tobacco, instruments, bearings, wax, locomotives, glass, plumbing equipment, bakery products, and beer provide a further sampling of the tremendous diversity of manufacturing industries which Schoolmen have come to head. As evidence, the following became chief executives: E.J. Marsh, '21, Niagara Packers Ltd; O.D. Johnston, '23, Gooderham and Worts Ltd; Norman E. Russell, '24, Aluminum Goods Ltd; V.B. King, '25, Timberjack Machines Ltd; John M. Keith, '29, Imperial Tobacco Co of Canada Ltd; E. Jack W. Sheare, '31, Taylor Instrument Companies of Canada Ltd; James W. Fry, '37, Torrington Co Ltd; David Aziz, '45, International Waxes Ltd; H.D. Allan, '46, Worthington (Canada) Ltd; and V.C. German, '50, Pilkington Glass Ltd. Harold W. Blakely, '50, an engineering and business graduate, attained the presidency of Crane at the age of 37, ten years after graduation. Three years later he was president of Consolidated Bakeries and a year after that of Carling Breweries.

Today, over 60 per cent of Canada's labour force is not in manufacturing but in some form of service industry. And, since the mid-1950s, as we have seen, engineers too have been moving rapidly out of manufacturing and into the service sector, which includes the consulting engineer. The 1971 Directory of Ontario Professional Engineers showed a thousand Toronto graduates registered as consultants. These and other graduates who are consultants have contributed mightily to the building of Canada and other countries.

Other graduates of the Faculty have made their mark in a wide variety of service areas. In banking and finance, R.M. Thomson, '55, has climbed to the presidency of the Toronto-Dominion Bank. L.G. Mills, '11, and G.R.P. Bongard, '49, head stockbroking firms bearing their names, while in venture financing, D'Alton L. Sinclair, '49, rose to president of Charterhouse Canada Ltd.

Another success story started when W.I.M. Turner, Jr, '51, went on a holiday nine years ago and came back to find himself president of a construction company where he had never worked. He had just joined Power Corporation of Canada Ltd, and while away from home had been chosen to straighten out management difficulties at one of the company's fourteen subsidiaries, Inspiration Construction. Turner did his housekeeping so well that he became known as a top trouble shooter and management expert. Three years later he was appointed president of the multi-billion dollar parent corporation.

In publishing, B.M. Thall, '45, became vice-president of the Toronto *Star*; and Herbert M. McManus, '23, editor of *Saturday Night*. The hotel industry has not escaped Schoolmen – H. Spencer Clark, '24, is president of the Guild Inn near Toronto. The country's two retail giants also have felt the impact of Toronto engineers. G. Allen Burton, a Schoolman from 1933 to 1935, was president of Simpsons Ltd and now is chairman of the board. O.D. Vaughan, '17, was a vice-president of the T. Eaton Co; he was also chairman of the board of governors of the University of Toronto from 1969 to 1971.

Systems engineering and computers, as new growth areas in the service industries, have brought more recent graduates to the fore. Jack B. Levine, '63, pioneered in the use of computers in educational planning while working on his doctorate at Toronto. He was a founder of the Systems Research Group which serves many educational institutions on both sides of the Canadian-u.s. border. Warren D. Beamish, '64, was one of the early entrepreneurs in the computer utility business, creating Computel Systems Ltd.

Toronto engineers have served all three levels of government – a few as politicians, many as civil servants. William J. Browne, '19, who took up law after engineering, was a member of the Newfoundland cabinet before that province joined Confederation, and later solicitor-general in the Diefenbaker government.

Another engineer-turned-lawyer, C. Fraser Elliott, '11, served from 1932 to 1946 as deputy minister of national revenue – Canada's chief tax collector. Then he switched to diplomacy and was Canadian ambassador to Chile for five years before being appointed high commissioner to Australia. N.F. Parkinson, '13, also became a federal deputy minister, in the Department of Soldier's Civil Re-establishment from 1920 to 1927.

The cheques that Toronto engineers wrote to the Receiver General of Canada during the 1960s were cashed by a fellow Schoolman, Robert B. Bryce, '32, son of the R.A. Bryce met earlier. As Canada's No. 1 mandarin, Bryce has over the past decade or longer probably been the country's most important and influential civil servant. After receiving his B A SC, he studied under the famous British economist, John Maynard Keynes, then joined the finance department and quickly rose to be assistant deputy minister and secretary to the Treasury Board. When J.W. Pickersgill resigned as clerk of the privy council and secretary to the cabinet, Bryce replaced him and served in this position under three prime ministers – St Laurent, Diefenbaker, and Pearson. In 1963 the new finance minister, Walter Gordon, demanded Bryce's services as deputy minister and receiver general, a position he held for seven years.

At the provincial level, John B. Cronyn, '47, as head of the Committee on Government Productivity, is restructuring the entire system of government and the public sector in Ontario. This is a part-time job: he is the senior vice-president of Labatt's.

Among many far-reaching changes, Cronyn's committee recommended the creation in 1972 of a number of new super-ministries in the policy field. The first deputy minister of one of these – social development – is Douglas T. Wright, '49. Previously, as first full-time chairman of the Committee on University Affairs, he had been 'Mr University' in Ontario during the explosive expansion in post-secondary education in the late 1960s, and one of the architects of university formula financing. As chairman of the Commission on Post-Secondary Education, he drafted policies, many of them quite radical, designed to bring Ontario higher education into the twenty-first century. Earlier, Wright was the first dean of engineering at the University of Waterloo which, through its co-operative program, now has the largest undergraduate engineering school in Canada.

Toronto spawned many other educators who went on to head engineering schools. J.W. Hodgins, '38, founded the faculty at McMaster University; in 1970, with Philip A. Lapp, '50, he completed a comprehensive study and plan for engineering education in Ontario, published under the title, *Ring of Iron*. Hodgins was succeeded as dean at McMaster by L.W. Shemilt, '41.

F.A. De Marco, '42, founded the engineering faculty at the University of Windsor and was its first dean. Later he became vice-president, academic. Maurice Adelman, '37, is head of chemical engineering at Windsor.

R.J. Uffen, '49, now is dean of engineering at Queen's University, after a short brilliant career as a federal civil servant – first as chairman of the Defence Research Board, then as director of the Science Secretariat before it became the Ministry of State for Science and Technology. A geophysicist, he was principal of University College, University of Western Ontario before entering government service in 1967.

Engineering at the University of Western Ontario was started in 1954 by L.S. Lauchland, '34. The present dean is A.I. Johnson, '46, a chemical engineer who had taught at Toronto and McMaster.

Carleton University's engineering faculty was started by John Ruptash, '50, an aeronautical engineer who has since become dean of graduate studies.

As might be expected, the past five Toronto deans were also Schoolmen: Brig-Gen C.H. Mitchell, '92 (1919-41), C.R. Young, '03 (1941-49), K.F. Tupper, '29 (1949-54), R.R. McLaughlin, '22 (1954-66), and James M. Ham, '43 (1966-73). So is the new dean, Bernard Etkin, '41.

Outside Ontario, John A. Stiles, '07, was the dean of applied science at the University of New Brunswick. He was better known to many Canadians, however, as chief executive commissioner of the Boy Scouts

Association of Canada – a post he held from its creation in 1930 to 1946. At the other end of the country, W.M. Armstrong, '37, was dean of applied science at the University of British Columbia, and now is deputy president.

When Ontario created eighteen Colleges of Applied Arts and Technology in 1967, the presidents of three were Schoolmen: J.K. Bradford, '32, at Loyalist College in Belleville; R.C. Quittenton, '43, at St Clair College in Windsor, and R.C. Short, '49, at St Lawrence College in Kingston. The first principal of Ryerson Polytechnical Institute – forerunner of the CAATS – was Howard H. Kerr, '22.

F.S. Rutherford, '14, spent his career with the Ontario Department of Education and ended up as deputy minister of education from 1946 to 1951. Other Toronto engineering graduates have headed universities – William G. Tamblyn, '45, Lakehead University, and William C. Winegard, '49, the University of Guelph. Winegard, a noted metallurgist, taught at Toronto before moving to Guelph.

Another member of the University of Guelph, as professor of international relations, is C. Willson Woodside, '29, who was a national figure during the second world war as a news analyst on the CBC. After graduation Woodside joined the Faculty at Toronto, and wrote for *Harper's, Maclean's,* and *Saturday Night* before becoming foreign editor of the latter publication in 1940. He attended the birth of the United Nations and was for many years national director of the United Nations Association in Canada. In 1962 he was elected vice-president of the World Federation of UN Associations.

While Woodside's name was becoming a household word during the war, L.R. Thomson, '06, was dodging publicity. A successful Montreal consultant and McGill University professor, he fought the Germans as a sort of long-distance Scarlet Pimpernel. He was responsible for much of the organization of the escape from under the Nazi noses of more than five hundred Polish engineers and technicians, and their subsequent employment in Canada. He also toured the United States persuading millionaires to sell their yachts to the ship-hungry Royal Canadian Navy. Later Thomson arranged for supplies of Canadian uranium, thorium, and other materials for the research that led to the atomic bomb.

Literally thousands of engineering alumni served in the armed forces in both world wars. While not the highest-ranking, Col H.G. (Spike) Thompson, '22, was one of the most significant. He had been a naval pilot in the first world war. As the second approached, he organized and commanded the First Canadian Reserve Army Field Workshop, and went active with it in 1939. Later he earned the title of 'Daddy' of the Royal Canadian Electrical and Mechanical Engineers, whose formation he supervised overseas.

Many of the graduates already mentioned for other reasons achieved distinction with the services during the wars. Others chose the armed forces as a permanent career. Among the latter were Maj-Gen W.H.S. Macklin, '23, who retired as adjutant-general in 1954 to become a noted defence policy critic, and Brig J.L.R. Parsons, '01, who organized and directed relief camps for the unemployed in New Brunswick during the depression. Others who made it to the senior ranks of the Canadian Defence Forces include A.C. Spencer, '07; Max M. Hendrick, '32; Victor S.J. Millard, '34; and Clare L. Annis, '36, who is now general manager of Canadian Patents and Development Ltd.

Backing Canada's armed forces through the development of new weapons, the Defence Research Board has gained worldwide recognition for its inventions and contributions to Western strength. Its chairman from 1956 to 1967 was A.H. Zimmerman, '24; he was succeeded by another Toronto engineering graduate, R.J. Uffen, '49.

Today, increasing emphasis is being placed on research and development in the private sector. The Ontario Research Foundation acts as a research department for literally thousands of small companies in the province and beyond, through separate contract projects. The president of ORF is William R. Stadelman, '41, and the director of research was for some time W.M. Campbell, '38.

Larger companies normally have their own research facilities, and Toronto engineering alumni play a key role in managing them. The wide diversity of their activity may be seen in a few examples. Leon J. Rubin, '38, a chemical engineer, became research director for Canada Packers Ltd. J.A. Carr, '41, is general manager of the Dunlop Research Centre. The research director of the Ontario Paper Co Ltd in Thorold, Ontario, is David Craig, '43. Frank W. Melvanin, '44, manages the research and development division of Eldorado Nuclear Ltd. More recent graduates who have become research managers include Byron B. Goodfellow, '53, IBM Canada Ltd; R.A. Bergman, '55, Falconbridge Metallurgical Laboratories; James M. Steward, '56, Dupont of Canada Ltd, and Noel G. Thomas, '57, Dofasco.

There have been some great success stories involving Toronto graduates in industrial research. J.W. Powlesland, '35, was the inventor and developer of 'air curtains' for the controlled flow of fumes and dust; he now heads a firm bearing his name that is exploiting the technique.

The extendable antennas first used on Canada's Alouette satellite were in large part the work of other Toronto graduates. Over a thousand of these

STEM (Storable Tubular Extendable Member) antennas have since been launched into space in Canadian, American, French, British, German, Japanese, and even Russian spacecraft. Originally conceived by G.J. Klein, '28, at NRC, the concept was developed and perfected at de Havilland's Special Products and Applied Research Division, later Spar Aerospace Products Ltd. Mainly responsible for the design and subsequent development was E. Groskopfs, '55.

The U.S. spaceflight program has used the STEM antenna on all three manned vehicles – Mercury, Gemini, and Apollo.At NASA one of the top technical posts was held by J.A. Chamberlin, '36, formerly design chief of the Avro Arrow, until its cancellation in 1959.

Few space engineers have been as bold and as imaginative as G.V. Bull, '48. He stacked two 140-ton 16-inch naval guns end-to-end at a launching site in Barbados and vertically fired 300-pound, equipment-laden projectiles to probe the stratosphere. The ultimate aim of HARP (High Altitude Research Program) is to launch payloads into orbit by cannon. Upon termination of Canadian support, Bull moved to the United States part-time, where his company is doing ballistics work for the armed forces.

U.S. military demands for better surveillance equipment sparked another development at Spar Aerospace. Using advanced types of infrared detectors, two graduates from the Class of 1965 – H.S. Kerr and R.M. Penrose – have developed several types of remote sensing systems that can be applied to resource surveys as well as defence.

Another graduate of 1950, Fred M. Longstaff, made important contributions in the computer field while at Ferranti-Packard Ltd. He conceived the FP 6000 – the first time-shared computer in history – and designed the related software. His work in Canada later formed the basis of the present British computer industry.

Still another member of the Class of 1950, Colin A. McLaurin, is applying his engineering skills in the medical field. He is director of prosthetics research at the Ontario Crippled Children's Centre.

Schoolmen are working at the cutting edge of new technology. For example, at York University, A.I. Carswell, '56, is using lasers to probe the atmosphere for pollutants and meteorological data. The technique will have commercial significance. At the University of Toronto Institute for Aerospace Studies, John W. Locke '64, is employing lasers for an entirely different purpose – to produce high-quality colour photographs from data received by sensors aboard resource satellites. There is a worldwide market for his laser-beam image recorder.

The mobility of engineers into other professions suggests that some have viewed their days at School as a general education. Several entered law and religion. Three members of the Class of 1915, for example, became lawyers – E.V. McKague, R.E. Laidlaw, and I.M. Macdonnell. After distinguished service in the first world war, McKague attended Osgoode Hall, graduating in 1921, and entered legal practice. Laidlaw practised with the firm of McCarthy and McCarthy and then joined the CNR before being called to the bench in 1943 as a judge of the Appeal Court in Ontario. With Dean C.R. Young, he was co-author of a work on engineering law used as a text-book in Canadian and U.S. universities. Macdonnell also became a judge of the York County Court, and was active in municipal politics as an alder-man in Toronto's Ward 4 in 1926 and 1927. (Another Schoolman, J.J. Hanna, '14, proved that you don't have to study law to enter civic politics. After an active engineering career with Imperial Oil, he became an alder-man in Calgary). Engineering graduates of more recent vintage who became lawyers are J.R. Cavanagh, '44, a patent attorney in Toronto, and A.K. Meen, QC, '46, who has served in key posts in the Ontario Municipal Electric Association.

Other Schoolmen turned to the ministry as a career. Among them have been D.E. Raymer, '36, and E.P. Miller, '46. A.M. Reid, president of the permanent executive of the famous Class of 1923, first served for thirty-five years with Bell Telephone before he entered the ministry of the Anglican Church.

Toronto's engineers have contributed significantly in various ways to the cultural fabric of our nation. Kenneth H.J. Clarke, '36, a vice-president of International Nickel, served as chairman of the board of governors and president of the Stratford Festival Foundation of Canada. Martin Baldwin, '13, was curator of the Art Gallery of Toronto from 1932 to 1947, and then its director until he retired in 1960.

It has been said that engineering and literature don't mix, but R.A. Boorne, '48, while carrying on his regular duties as a professor of engineer-ing at Mount Allison University, turned out plays for the CBC. His best known was 'The Day of the Dodo,' a ninety-minute 1962 television drama based on a major aircraft project that collapsed.

One of the best-known figures in Canada's national sport, Maj Conn Smythe, fiery head of the Toronto Maple Leaf hockey club, earned his B A SC in 1920. He has called himself 'the second worst engineer to graduate,' without specifying who was the worst. In the year after graduat-ing he started a contracting firm specializing in sand and gravel. Five years later he helped to organize the New York Rangers, then with others bought the Toronto St Pats hockey club which he promptly renamed the Maple Leafs and built for them a 14,000-seat arena as a permanent home – Maple Leaf Gardens.

While Smythe was watching for marksmen with the puck, Gil Boa, '46, had his eye on a different target. As Canada's No 1 sharpshooter with a rifle, he won international and Olympic medals. Boa now manages the Swan Wooster Engineering offices in St Catharines, Ontario.

School's cultural influence extends south of the border. R.P. Johnson, '14, was general superintendent of the American Museum of Natural History. J.L. Skinner, '16, has put on a series of one-man watercolour shows in Florida, Georgia, and Nassau. C.W. Hancock, '18, became a well-known horticulturist, winning many awards for his prize orchids and becoming president of the American Orchid Society.

The kaleidoscopic pattern of engineering careers shows the Schoolmen's tremendous diffusion into positions of leadership from which they have managed and controlled the building of the nation. In one hundred years, Toronto engineering graduates have helped significantly to mould Canada. When the School of Practical Science was started a century ago, industry was in its infancy. The mills were powered by water and steam, grinding the foodstuffs and weaving the textiles necessary for the frugal life of the country. Sawmills and woodworking mills were of the simplest design. There were no steel mills, no pulp and paper mills, practically no mining, and no electric power or light; there was telegraph communication but no telephone. Gas and oil were in use for lighting, and waterworks and other municipal works of a kind existed, but the streetcars were still drawn by horses. Railways had been built and were a-building, but the oldest had been operating for only twenty years. There were some small St Lawrence canals and the second of the Welland Canals was under construction. Some steamers plied the lakes, but most ships still were moved by wind and sail.

What a contrast today! In November 1972, the world's first domestic communications satellite was placed in operation by Canada's Telesat Corporation. Anik will help to open the Arctic and unite the isolated communities of this country with its densely populated regions. It symbolizes the tremendous strides Canada has made, both in the worldwide technological community and in the application of technology to social development. It should come as no surprise that another Toronto engineering graduate, R.F. Chinnick, '46, headed the Anik team. As Telesat's engineering vice-president, he viewed the launch with somewhat more than casual interest – five ... four ... three ... two ... one ... swoosh!

The author is indebted to the exhaustive efforts of Mrs Beverley Roberts, who did the research and endless digging for data that made this chapter possible.

JAMES M. HAM

Images of the past and future

I visualize the Faculty of Applied Science and Engineering within the University of Toronto as being in the outer of the three concentric rings shown in figure 1. The inner circle contains the core of the university. The Faculty of Applied Science and Engineering forms part of the peripheral ring of professional schools surrounding the inner annular rings. Outside the peripheral ring lie the profession, industry, and society at large.

The Lapp report[1] on the state of engineering education in Ontario noted that, in comparison with other institutions, the interplay between Engineering and the remainder of the University of Toronto was distinctively strong. From its independent development in downtown Toronto as the School of Practical Science (School of Technology) in 1873 to its integration into the university under its present name in 1906, the Faculty may be said to have followed a path dictated by political decision and not by institutional choice.[2] Since 1906, despite fireworks, perennially involving students and occasionally administrators, relationships with the university as a whole have gradually developed to their present healthy state. This interplay must remain a distinctive element if the university is to respond constructively to the increasing tensions created by a technological society.

1 P.A. Lapp et al., *Ring of Iron* (Toronto: Committee of Presidents of Ontario Universities, 1971)
2 C.R. Young, *Early Engineering Education at Toronto* (Toronto: University of Toronto Press, 1958)

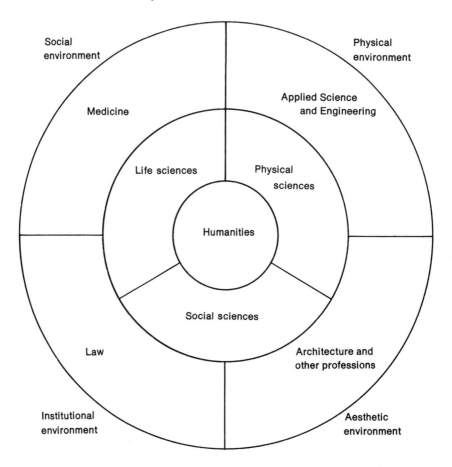

Figure 1
Applied Science and Engineering in the university

At the outer interfaces there is at present criticism that we have been too celibate of mind and curriculum and not heedful enough of the working needs of Canadian industy and of the practising engineer. Massive importation of technology is a continuing fact of Canadian life. Coupled with this technological colonialism are the stresses of intense urbanization and the social unease of a bicultural nation being propelled continentally into post-industrialism. The term *post-industrialism* is used to characterize a society in which more persons deliver services to one another than produce primary materials or manufactured goods. In Canada today only one in ten of us works in the forests, fields, mines, and fisheries. Three in ten work in manufacturing and construction. The remaining six work in the service sector, which includes education, government, and retail sales. In 1873 such a society was not conceived of.

What, then, will and should the Faculty become? Alvin Toffler has made it popular at the moment to discuss the problems of institutions and persons in terms of discontinuous shock-waves of change. Yet change must be perceived within a reference frame, content must be seen within a context, and magnitudes must be read on scales of measurement.

Engineering has its invariant features and these are historically transmitted. Let me start with these features and in so doing relate briefly the words *engineering, technology,* and *science.*

In a presidential address given to the Canadian Society of Civil Engineers on 27 January 1909, Dean John Galbraith said:

> In tracing backwards the history of the engineer to classical times, two words stand out with marked prominence – μηχανή and *ingenium*. The root idea of the former is contrivance, resource, ways, means: of the latter, nature, intelligence, ingenuity ... The antiquity of the words and the continued application of their derivatives down to the present day to the same set of ideas are evidence that the art and craft of the engineer are not of yesterday nor the outcome of modern conditions.

To design, to synthesize, to organize, to manage technical resources in a socially useful and economical manner is the *invariant* central role of the professional engineer. The core of engineering education will continue to be determined by this role. In this regard it must be understood that technical means or technologies are not simply the consequence of the application of pure science. As Polanyi has carefully argued: 'Technology comprises all acknowledged *operational* principles and endorses the purposes which they serve ... the class of things defined by a common operational principle cannot be even approximately specified in terms of physics and chemistry.'[3]

Physics and chemistry cannot tell us that an aeroplane is an aeroplane and much less whether it is a Canadian bush plane. In designing technical means, engineering is concerned with human purpose and does not stand simply on the shoulders of science. This point has always been crucial to an understanding of the role of the pure sciences in engineering education and practice. The process of engineering education is concerned with engendering profiles of comprehension within this set of ideas.

While the concept of the engineer's professional role has remained constant, its context has changed dramatically in the past century. (Its specific content of course changes daily.) The change in context has immensely extended the potential scope of engineering. Indeed, this increase in scope is now the primary influence altering the pattern of engineering education and it will continue to be in the foreseeable future. It is already inducing serious 'identity' stresses within the profession.

What have been the major events of contextual change for engineering in the century since this Faculty was founded? There have been three. Whitehead has described the first in *Science and the Modern World*: 'The greatest invention of the nineteenth century was the invention of the method of invention.' Although there is some disagreement as to when this 'event' occurred, there can be no doubt that, aided by the developing technological interdependence of science and engineering, the concept of consciously bridging the speculative arch from operational idea to marketable product has become firmly embedded in the industrial fabric of Europe and North America during the past fifty years. Much of the Industrial Revolution occurred in England with only negligible influence from the universities, but the new technical universities of Germany and the Massachusetts Institute of Technology in the USA may be regarded as reflections of Whitehead's insight.[4] For several decades there has been a persistent strengthening of studies in applied science within engineering education, a trend reinforced and accelerated by the social pressures for technological achievement in two world wars. The founding of the Engineering Physics program jointly by the Faculties of Arts and of Applied Science and Engineering in 1935 epitomizes this movement at Toronto. That program, renamed Engineering Science in 1964, is the major one of its kind in Canada and promises to remain a distinctive feature of engineering educa-

3 M. Polanyi, *Personal Knowledge* (New York: Harper, 1964), pp. 328-32
4 E. Ashby, *Technology and the Academics* (London: Macmillan, 1959)

tion at this university. Among its graduates are many of the leaders in Canadian engineering research and development.

Within this general trend, engineering education has often been slow to introduce a suitable compass of modern mathematics, physics, and chemistry into its curriculum. Now, however, we are sometimes accused of having gone too far. Certainly, the striking of a wise balance between design and analysis, between the comprehension of the operational principles and humane uses of technologies and the appreciation of basic scientific principles, will always remain a problem.

If the first major contextual change for engineering has been the interweaving of science with engineering, characterized by the acronym R & D, the second concerned the expansion of knowledge itself, and of accessibility to knowledge through our technological systems for the transportation and communication of goods, information, and persons. Electronic computers now form a singular part of these technological systems. Knowledge has become a parameter of social and economic 'state,' parallel in significance to the classical parameters of labour and capital. This phenomenon has many manifestations but is brilliantly implied in U Thant's statement:

The central stupendous truth about developed economies today is that they can have – in anything but the shortest run – the kind and scale of resources they decide to have. It is no longer resources that limit decisions. It is the decision that makes the resources. This is the fundamental revolutionary change – perhaps the most revolutionary man has ever known.

A distinctive part of this change is reflected in the development of patterns of systematic interaction between men and machines. In industrial automation, and indeed in most human institutions, the dominant problems often concern the flow of information rather than the technical performance of specific machines or processes. That is to say, in the interactive systems of modern industry and government, 'software' has become as important as 'hardware.' This phenomenon opens up an immense new scope for engineering as a profession, and one which has but partially been probed.

The Faculty responded to this second contextual evolution most significantly by introducing in 1948 the program in Engineering and Business, which was followed in 1961 by the establishment of the Department of Industrial Engineering. The current calendar of the Faculty defines that department's role as follows:

The modern view of Industrial Engineering is that of a field concerned with the analysis, design, improvement and operation of integrated systems of men, materials and equipment. This concept crystallized when it became clear that certain modern technical fields, including operational research, control theory, computer science, probability and statistics, system theory and human factors engineering, constituted a body of knowledge particularly useful in the operation and management of modern business, industry and government.

Today and in the future the systems approach of industrial engineering can be expected to thrive within the increasingly interactive context of post-industrial society.

The third major contextual change for engineering has been the social comprehension of what I shall call the *eco-quantum* effect, namely that man's activity on the surface of the earth is now exceeding thresholds of intensity that induce radical changes in the lived environment. These changes are characterized not only by physical pollution of air, soil, and water, but also by psycho-social stresses of concentrated urbanization and the rising cacophony of the media. Whereas classical definitions of the role of engineering have always referred to bending the forces of nature to the use and convenience of man, it is clear now that in a new sense engineering is deeply concerned with the consequences of man's activity itself. As our concepts of interaction and interdependence have been enlarged, as the scale of the systems we seek to design has grown, the distinction between the natural and the designed environment has lost its bucolic simplicity. This recognition will permeate the future development of engineering education, and perhaps all education.

In summary, then, the growing technological interdependence of science and engineering, the emergence of knowledge itself as a major parameter of socio-economic development, and the perception of man's environment as a complex of eco-systems, are the primary events within which one must view the development of the Faculty's programs now and in the future.

If the Engineering Science program initiated in 1935 reflected the first of those primary events, the recent massive growth in graduate studies and research reflects governmental acceptance of the second – that knowledge in itself is, and will be, a major propellant of socio-economic development. This growth – at Toronto and throughout Ontario – can be calibrated as follows. In 1962, when the Ford Foundation made the Faculty a grant of $2,325,000 over a five-year period, $735,000 of it for capital purposes, there were 229 graduate students. In 1971 the Faculty's annual rate of operating expenditure from external research grants and contracts was over $3 million, the graduate enrolment was 580, and the internal operating budget was about $6 million. In 1962-3 our graduate enrolment exceeded that of the eight other provincial engineering schools combined. By 1970 we represented but half of the graduate enrolment in the Ontario universities, seven of which were chartered by the provincial legislature in the period 1950-65. Our undergraduate enrolment of 2,200 in 1971 represented about one quarter of the provincial enrolment. Many of the operational problems of institutions develop with changes in size. My view is that the Faculty as a whole is now very much at the stage of 'critical mass' and should, except in a very few areas, place a sustained emphasis on quality and not on growth.

The development in other Canadian institutions of para-engineering programs for technologists and technicians deserves careful watching to ensure that national development is served by a balanced spectrum of talents. The lack of adequate para-engineering programs in Canada has until recently been serious. In most developing countries there continues to be a sad imbalance in this regard. The cause appears to be an overweening concern for the assumed prestige of academe.

While graduate studies and research in the established areas of aerospace, chemical, civil, electrical, industrial, mechanical, and metallurgical engineering have thrived during the recent past, new foci of research have been established on both interdepartmental and interfaculty bases. In major part their development reflects an intensified perception of the interaction of science, engineering, and technology and a concern for social consequences. Moreover, new government policies making contract funds available for particular mission-oriented tasks are now for the first time a factor in shaping research patterns in Canada. In the future they may have strong influence on the funding of engineering research, which to date has drawn its major sustenance from the National Research Council. Canada is only now edging its way towards a strategy for industrial development and a related policy for science and technology. It is sad that 'engineering' is rarely on the lips of our politicians.

Figure 2 shows the developing pattern of interactions in graduate studies and research between the Faculty of Applied Science and Engineering, the remainder of the University of Toronto, and other Ontario universities. A similar diagram could be drawn to characterize the interactions across departmental boundaries. In a modern multiversity, which is a microcosm of the post-industrial society, the patterns of intellectual identity are those of a complex molecule, between the atomic centres of which occur bonds of increasing diversity. An engineering school is and will be immensely

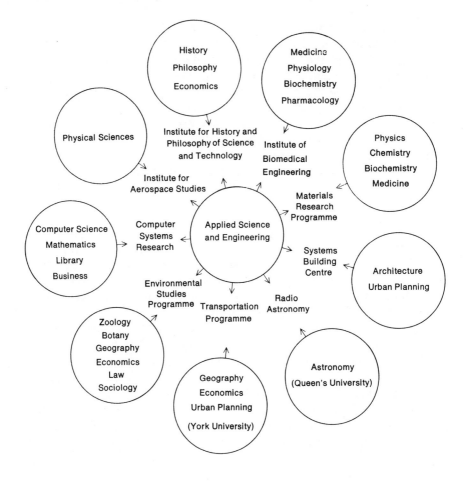

Figure 2
Interaction with the university in research and teaching

richer for living within and forming an active part of such an intellectual molecule. The Faculty played a significant role in developing each of the bonds shown in figure 2. One of these, the Institute for the History and Philosophy of Science and Technology, is in part a venture in recovering a humane historical sense of the technological context of our society.

Molecular models of the university convey much insight into likely arrangements of intellectual centres. Interdisciplinary studies are viable only as bonds of interaction between primary disciplinary identities, which commonly are departments. Proposed new faculties of interdisciplinary studies are contradictions in terms, for they would be faculties consisting of bonds without atoms to connect to.

One may, however, with such models envisage new conceptions of a 'college' as a seat of intellectual community; and from these I would propose that the Faculty of Applied Science and Engineering become the College of Applied Science and Engineering, attracting into its professional core a whole range of intellectual bonds within the molecular university. As such it would be a sub-molecule encompassing in the concern of its associated staff and students not only engineering and technology *per se* but also the undergirding human questions of means and ends. In this regard there is need to develop in the university a renewed sense of 'usefulness' – one that is not distorted into a form of 'politicized relevance.'

Ortega y Gasset has said in *Man and Crisis* that 'life is not to be lived for the sake of intelligence, science, culture, but the reverse; intelligence, science, culture have no other reality than that which accrues to them as tools for life.' The primacy of the university as a place of the intellect is not challenged by such a view, but some of the quality of conventional academic life may be. The current disenchantment of the public and of government with the myth of knowledge and hence with the universities can be met by a renewal of the wholeness of intellectual life in the multiversity. The professional faculties and not least Applied Science and Engineering have a role to play in the outer ring of figure 1. In particular, it is time to lay to rest the historical institutional unease about the propriety of engineering being in the university. Understanding something of how we may make sensitive and frugal uses of technology must surely be a part of the intellectual curiosity of any person who claims to be literate today.

Ancient technology was developed in many instances to support the decorative art of jewelry. And technology, like art, is always in advance of scientific understanding. Only recently, for example, have we come to understand how the ancient Chinese made metal mirrors. Perhaps we shall learn to conceive of the spacially embossed forms of cities as our jewels and their surrounds as our necklaces created by technologies of immense variety.

With the molecular multiversity there has come to the student greater freedom to choose subjects to be studied. One sometimes wonders if this phenomenon is not simply a reflection of greater consumer choice in a post-industrial society. Yet in engineering it is essential to preserve a distinctive profile of subjects of study which, taken together with practical experience acquired during the four undergraduate years, defines a *process* of education designed to develop a professional cast of mind. Testing of competence through examinations, design projects, and the like must remain part of professional attainment and of self-acceptance. The introduction of significant freedom of choice among the several non-technical curricular subjects has tended to 'privatize' the interest of the individual student in the humanistic context of his studies and hence to deter the working out of a professional consensus. I am led to ask whether the issues of ethics, law, social responsibility, and so on that confront the engineer cannot be articulated better within the concept of a 'college of engineering' than by the random wanderings of a student among the pages of university calendars.

The identification of suitable professional profiles of study, in essence the design of curricula, will continue to be a challenge, not least because the Canadian Council of Professional Engineers in 1972 initiated for the first time nation-wide procedures for accreditation of schools. I predict a measure of invariance of profile that will give the lie to the overstated alarm about obsolescence. Profile and context may be stable while content changes radically. Learning must be distinguished from the acquisition of mere facts. It is the process that is crucial.

If there is some reason for satisfaction with the general intellectual profile of our engineering programs and with their bonds to the inner university, there is need for concern and innovation regarding our bonds and service to the outer environment of Canadian industry, government, and society. The elements of this discussion are suggested by figure 3.

I referred earlier to an imputed celibacy in our undergraduate curriculum, which, to the extent that it is real, is created by three limitations: 1/ a chronic inadequacy of resources to provide effective laboratories for experimentation and project designs; 2/ the non-innovative character of a dominantly branch-plant regional industrial complex; 3/ our own lack of innovation and experimentation with the external bonds that parallel the inner bonds of figure 2.

The pattern of undergraduate registration reflects these problems.

Enrolments, which currently peak in Electrical Engineering and are lowest in Metallurgy and Materials Science, are determined by the choices of secondary school students who at best acquire a very limited appreciation of the economic and social problems of Canada's development. We have mounted a secondary school liaison program and this work will assume increasing importance in the future. While professional engineers have traditionally demonstrated their ability to move across the fictitious barriers of academic instruction, there is need in Canada for the achievement of enrolment patterns that bear closer relation to true national needs. A new undergraduate division of study in Applied Earth Sciences and Engineering – linking together civil engineering, metallurgy, geology, and geophysics to provide branch programs in engineering geology, mineral exploration, and mineral engineering – is now being shaped. It is designed to serve the mining and construction industries with extended scope. Will it attract the students Canada needs?

Is there a larger role for women in the profession? In 1920 there were four women students in a Faculty total of 819, while in 1971 there were thirty-five out of 2,238. Women are succeeding in every branch of the profession and should in the future play a much more significant role.

If enrolment patterns are not now well balanced, what of the quality of the technical and professional elements of the undergraduate experience as distinct from the elements of applied and engineering sciences? There is need to renew and diversify these by innovation within, and by the establishment of new forms of molecular bonds with persons and facilities in industry and government. We have begun making use of external facilities by having metallurgy students study pilot-plant mineral separation at the Ontario Research Foundation at Sheridan Park. This is an approximation to 'clinical' experience, a generic development which should be encouraged in engineering education. Co-operative laboratory instruction with Ryerson Polytechnical Institute may prove mutually beneficial.

The Faculty might well create a new category of affiliated Staff drawn from industry and government laboratories under the title of 'professional associate.' These persons might come to the Faculty to discuss case studies involving social, technical, economic, and environmental factors, and receive and supervise individual students in project work for limited periods of clinical internship. Part-time staff from industry have already been used in small numbers and case-study seminars are not uncommon. What is needed is a coherent development of such bonds, not in the conventional academic forms of part-time lecturing and the slotting of 'co-operative' education but rather in an elective and negotiable way based on

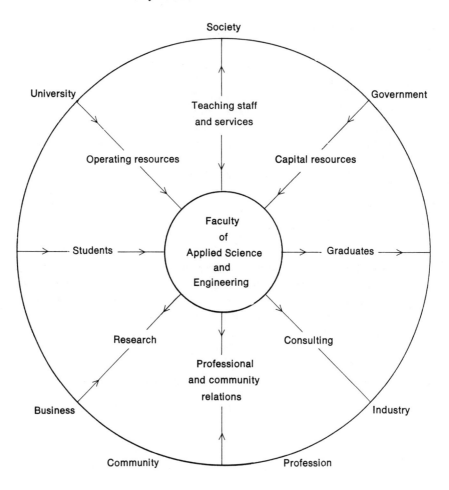

Figure 3
Interaction with the environment

the professional involvement of our staff with industry and society at large. The co-operative funding of such bonds will present problems that must be solved.

In a country such as Canada, which is sadly deficient in industrial innovation, it is essential that our engineering schools become active in transferring to industry expertise and ideas which will stimulate innovation. While there is widespread national concern for this issue, it is not clear that the process of innovation is well understood. One myth is that increased governmental funding of research and development will stimulate industrial innovation. The facts appear to be that the essential ingredient for innovation is the presence of nuclei of entrepreneurially minded management having access to venture capital. R & D then becomes a logical need in the overall process of delivering new goods or services. The continued absence of a national strategy for industrial development keeps us in a state of technological colonialism. A happy exception to this state is to be found in the Canadian nuclear power program.

Clearly, engineering is but part of the process of innovation, but I believe that graduate students in particular should be exposed to the whole process and I like to think that Engineering at Toronto will increasingly develop an entrepreneurial bent. Undergraduate students must be given a deeper comprehension of the economic, social, and industrial environment of their province and their country. The innovative atmosphere is not an isolated one and cumulative small improvements in existing systems can be as important as radical novelty.

What, then, can the Faculty deliver across the bonds to the outer environment of figure 3? Much more than is currently expected by either government or the public. In contrast, in the USA the spawning of new knowledge-based industries, such as electronics and plastics, has thrust universities into the foreground of publicly recognized resources for science, engineering, and technology.

Figure 3 suggests the significant flows between the Faculty and the outer environment. Let us consider the flow of ideas and information. While professional consulting by individuals with specialized competence and experience continues on a modest scale in a long tradition, there has recently arisen, first in Chemical Engineering, the concept of team consulting in which substantial numbers of staff members together undertake commitments to assist companies and government departments. Private professional consultants have objected on occasion and argued that all such services should be delivered through them as the primary agent. While consulting to consultants is a desirable form of professional activity, the service of Faculty staff to industry and government should not be so constrained. The great majority of our work involves the interpretation of new possibilities for materials and technologies related to our research programs, interpretations of which by their special nature are not available through private consultants. The scope for such work has been vastly expanded by the distinctive molecular bonds of our work to the inner university, as suggested in figure 2. New forms of composite materials for modular construction, novel processes to convert industrial effluents into useful products, or holographic radar techniques to measure the thickness of Arctic ice, are not transferred simply as expertise but within a context of social, economic, and intellectual development. Such work does not replace but supplements the consultant's traditional role of providing expert advice on existing problems. Just as taxable profits are not made just on paper, our competence to interact with industry does not derive from teaching in the classroom.

There is a pressing need for deeper understanding between industry and our engineering schools about what each can and must expect of the other. Canada remains an underdeveloped country in this regard. One direction in which progress can be made is by transforming the character of continuing education. Let us admit that the conventional approach, of offering selected slices of the standard academic pie, has served few engineers well. Let us also admit that it has done little to help tax-paying industry understand how patterns of research provide an essential sustaining stimulus for an engineering school.

In the future we must serve not only individuals but the leadership of enterprises. We should do so by sharing 'modules of comprehension' generated by teams of staff interacting with groups of persons from society. The teams should generally involve more than engineers and scientists. Opportunities therefore exist in such continuing education for new mosaics of association within the university. The approach to instruction might be based on generic themes such as the technologies of new materials, methods of modelling processes, the interaction of men and machines, or the interplay between organizational structures and information systems, with interaction coming out of the experience of both staff and 'student.' With sequences of such modules, the horizons of both industry and university will be stretched. We need seminars to stimulate comprehension of the context in which each sector performs its role. The Master of Engineering program initiated in 1966, which focuses on the working experience of the student, was a first step towards such a philosophy of interactive career education. But degrees need not be an ingredient of continuing education and in general should not be. The essential element is the interlacing and challenging of different experiences.

Information systems which facilitate the posing of questions by industry to the university and by the university to industry will come, and they will not be dominated by conventional libraries. They will be distinguished by innovative structures for directing attention to selected subject issues wherever the data and ideas may best be located – in persons, institutions, books, films, computer structures. Each specialized technology, such as the book alone or the computer alone, is self-limiting.

Only molecular systems of men and machines will serve the needs of persons for access and response to information. Students of the Faculty have recently conceived of an Engineering Centre within the university which could form the focus of a molecular structure for continuing education characterized by scintillating bonds to diverse atomic centres in industry and society. It is an imaginative concept calling for entrepreneurship by industry, the university, and government.

If Canadian engineering schools are duty bound, as they are, to exert themselves with fresh vigour to serve the national needs, they must also share more widely in helping the underdeveloped countries. The Faculty began this role in the sixties by guiding the development of one of India's new regional engineering colleges over a period of three years. We are now exploring interactive support programs with Chile and Cuba. And among our Canadian-born students a few are acquiring fluency in Chinese within a curricular profile which – while tied to engineering – is perhaps a good *general* education for a post-industrial world.

I have discussed some facets of the Faculty within the rings of the university. At every interface there is change of context and scale. But as we enter a second century we shall do well to heed the words of Dean John Galbraith: 'The art and craft of the engineer are not of yesterday nor the outcome of modern conditions.' Indeed they are part of the phenomenon of man, in which the Old Testament charter of the engineer, 'to replenish the earth and subdue it,' has all too fully been realized. In the future, Engineering must serve the wiser purposes of man.

Contributors

B. ETKIN, '41, has for many years been a professor in the Institute for Aerospace Studies, and was chairman of Engineering Science from 1967 to 1972. In July 1973 he became the Faculty's eighth dean.

JAMES M. HAM, '43, was dean of the Faculty from 1966 to 1973, and before that was chairman of the Department of Electrical Engineering.

ROBIN S. HARRIS is professor of Higher Education in the University of Toronto and University Historian.

ALAN HEISEY, '51, has for some years been associated with Southam Business Publications, currently as general manager of *Daily Commercial News and Construction Record*.

P.B. HUGHES, a graduate of McGill University, was for many years professor of Mechanical Engineering, and now is secretary to the Board of Examiners, Association of Professional Engineers of the Province of Ontario.

PHILIP A. LAPP, '50, is a consultant. He is co-author of two studies of engineering education, *Ring of Iron*, and *Careers of Engineering Graduates 1920-70* (the latter a Centennial project of the Faculty of Applied Science and Engineering).

W.G. MAC ELHINNEY, '40, is professor of Chemical Engineering in the Faculty of Applied Science and Engineering.

ERIC J. MIGLIN, '72, was president of the Engineering Society in 1971-2, and in the following year president of the Students' Administrative Council of the University of Toronto.

IAN MONTAGNES is general editor of the University of Toronto Press.

A.M. REID, permanent president of the Class of 1923, after a career in the Bell Telephone Company was ordained an Anglican minister.

R.S. SEGSWORTH, a member of the redoubtable Class of 1935, is professor of Electrical Engineering in the Faculty.

W.W. WALKER, '50, is a former president of the Engineering Alumni Association, was for some years on the staff of the University's Department of Alumni Affairs, and now is teaching at George Brown College of Applied Arts and Technology.

Photographic credits

We are especially grateful to the many alumni of the Faculty who responded to a request for old photographs and dug into their files and albums to send examples for use in this book; and we regret that only a small proportion of these pictures could be fitted into the available space. Thanks also are due to the staff of the University of Toronto News Bureau and the University of Toronto Archives, and to Professors G. Ross Lord and H.R. Rice. For purposes of photo identification in the following list, the two photographic inserts are imagined to have page numbers, in each case running from 1 to 16.

Section 1: School of yesteryear (following page 56). Page 1, courtesy of Mrs Grace M. Craig. Page 2, Public Archives of Canada, courtesy of the Bell family. Page 3, A.A. Kinghorn. Pages 4, 6, 7, 8 top, 9, 10, 11, and 13 bottom, University of Toronto Archives. Page 8 bottom, University News Bureau. Page 12, top and bottom left, W.L. Bradley; bottom right, C.J. Marshall. Page 13, top, C.J. Marshall. Pages 14 and 15, top four pictures, W.L. Bradley; bottom left, Roy F. Gross; bottom right, R.J. Richardson. Page 16, Jack Marshall.

Section 2: School today (following page 88). Page 1, Panda. Pages 2, 3, 5, and 7, Jack Marshall. Pages 4, 8, 11, 13, 14, and 15, Robert Lansdale. Page 6, Herb Nott. Page 9, PM Productions. Page 10, Bill Dowkes. Page 12, top, H.J. Leutheusser; bottom, Bell and Rice.

Index